JOY

BLOSSOMS
Among the Thorns

Wyatt & Sons books may be ordered through booksellers or by contacting:

WYATT & SONS PUBLISHERS, LLC
399 Lakeview Dr. W.
Mobile, Alabama 36695
www.wyattpublishing.com

Because of the dynamic nature of the Internet, any web address or links contained in this book may have changed since publication and may no longer be valid.

Cover design by: Mark Wyatt
Interior design by: Mark Wyatt
ISBN 13:978-1-954798-24-3

This book is also available at amazon.com, barnesandnoble.com, and other online retailers.

Printed in the United States of America

Joy

BLOSSOMS
Among the Thorns

Book Two in the series
THE FRUIT OF THE SPIRIT:
THE PRODUCE OF GOD'S PRESENCE

by
SUSAN SLADE
and
SUSIE HALE

WS

WYATT & SONS
PUBLISHERS, LLC
Mobile, Alabama

DEDICATIONS

When we were thinking of someone to write a Foreword for this book, I told Susan that Bro. Jimmy Draper was one the most joy-filled people I had ever known. How blessed we are that after reading the entire book, he graciously wrote the foreword. I dedicate this book to Brother Jimmy because as my pastor for about thirteen years at First Baptist Euless, he was a major spiritual influence in my life. His expository teaching instilled in me the need to investigate the context of any passage I study. His habit of sending hand-written thank you notes for any act of service (even sending him a poem based on his sermon) reminded me to be thankful not only to people but to the Lord. I'll never forget him saying about inspiring or exciting Scripture passages, "Now if that doesn't light your fire, your wood's wet!"

I also dedicate this book to the memory of Jessica Muncie Gunnels (1986-2023). I had the privilege of being Jessica's teacher for both first and second grades at Glenview Christian School. Even as a young child she understood that she had cystic fibrosis, and that even though managing her health was time consuming, CF did not dictate who she was. She lived a life full of the love of her Lord Jesus and the joy of knowing Him intimately. She was definitely an example of Joy blossoming among the thorns of life! She is now basking in the presence of her first love, the Lord Jesus Christ.

Susie Hale

I dedicate this book to my Savior and Lord, Jesus Christ, who is the genesis of genuine joy, not happiness based on circumstances but an overall well-being and wholeness that is not shaken by the ups and downs, flowers and thorns, we experience in our earth-suits.

I dedicate this book, also, to the memory of two (among many in my life) who exemplified the joy found in Jesus. My former pastor and Bonus Dad, Doug White, who went to be with the Lord in December of 2022, was the epitome of tackling the tests and trials of life head on while holding on to the joy of the Lord triumphantly. He always had a glint of love and joy in his eye and a hint of mischief in his smile. The fire of the Holy Spirit coursed through him when he preached the Word boldly. His wife, Larie, served at his side with grace. She is still compassionate, discerning, and engaging; and I treasure her as a mom in the faith.

Dee White (who was married to a Doug White but was not related to Doug White in the preceding paragraph except by the blood of Jesus) seemed to always be effervescent with joy. Her bright smile could light up a room. I remember Mama Dee dancing enthusiastically with her son, Jon, at his wedding reception even though she was in her late 80's at the time. Mama Dee truly danced through life to the rhythm of her Savior's grace for His glory. Her relationship with Jesus infused her with an infectious, irresistible joy. Her relationship with Jesus infused her with an infectious, irresistible joy. She was pleased to see that I was exercising God's call on my life by writing these devotional books. She kept them on her kitchen table and would share her favorite pages with her friends. Hearing that the books brought her joy encourages me greatly.

Susan Slade

ACKNOWLEDGEMENTS

Cal McCarter (aka Pops) who first planted the idea of Susan writing a book about joy about 20 years ago. He is now with the Lord, but we still wanted to acknowledge the encouragement he gave.

Gail Meaux, Susan's English teacher in junior high and high school, who expanded her vocabulary and gave her a love for writing.

Richard Albin for creating the beautiful AI picture of the prickly pear cactus on the front cover and our photos on the back cover.

PJM board members – Dane and Dana Carr, Crystal Foster, Eric Little, Nick Miller and PJM Treasurer Rick Ivey.

PJM "Generous Gems" – Those who give regularly to support our ministry and "Jesus's Jewels" – those who consistently lift up Precious Jewels Ministries in prayer.

Mark Wyatt of Wyatt & Sons Publishers, for working patiently with us until a book is the best it can be.

Brother Jimmy Draper for writing the Foreword and giving us valuable feedback after reading the draft of the book.

Steve and Chelsea Landsee for their invaluable assistance in our final proofreading. Their attention to the most minute details helped us to make this book the best humanly possible.

"Team Uplift" – Dane and Dana Carr, Chelsea Landsee, Nick Shepard, and Zachary Sullivan who not only lift Susan physically into or out of her chair but also encourage and pray for us.

If the Lord leads you to contribute to our ministry via a monetary donation, you may do so via our website https://www.preciousjewelsministries.com by PayPal, credit card, or debit card. Or you can send funds via Venmo @Susan-PJM. You may also mail a check made out to Precious Jewels Ministries to P.O. Box 1343, Hurst, TX 76053.

Soli Deo Gloria!

FOREWORD

You have obtained one of the most remarkable books ever. It is a book about JOY & REJOICING. Now, that is not what makes it so significant. It is the source of these pages that is so impressive. This is a message about the joy of the Lord that is available to every believer. It was not written out of the good fortune of Susie Hale and Susan Slade. In fact, it was written in the midst of severe physical challenges that have destroyed other individuals in the past. From the amputation of Susan's legs in addition to the complications of cerebral palsy from her birth to the continual back pain that is debilitating for both of them, these two incredible women have experienced the Supernatural joy of the Lord. Rather than focusing on their severe physical challenges, their message is abounding and exciting as they describe the joy the Lord has placed in their hearts. Expressions like "Celebrate with Joy!," "Joy unrestrained," "effervescent Joy," "Exuberant, exhilarating celebration," "explosive rejoicing" and "extravagantly celebrate Him" are found throughout these pages. You will be blessed as you are lifted up to the Father in Joyful Praise. You will experience a view of Joy that does not often find its way in the midst of crushing obstacles. What Susie and Susan experience daily has made many to become bitter.

Not these two overcomers! It has only made them better and has brought them into the presence of the Lord with unbridled Joy and Thanksgiving. Your faith will be strengthened as you share their journey into heavenly rejoicing! Most of all you will be blessed with a new view of suffering and a fresh glimpse of our Lord Jesus Christ! You will never forget the source of their Joy and will never look at the circumstances of your own life in the same way again!

Jimmy Draper
President Emeritus, LifeWay

INTRODUCTION

Joy Blossoms Among the Thorns is book two in the series The Fruit of the Spirit: The Produce of God's Presence. The prickly pear cactus presents a great illustration of this truth. There among the cactus thorns bloom beautiful magenta flowers which in time become the dark pink prickly pear fruit which is thorny but edible! Life in our earth-suits is often difficult even on our "best days." However, pain or trials or times of mourning cannot rob us of our joy—that deep satisfaction and peace of knowing God is in control. Happiness can be fleeting and is circumstantial, but joy is a deep-seated contentment than can be known by all who trust in Jesus Christ as Savior and Lord. Our hope is that this book will help the reader realize the true joy that is present even when prickly thorns seem to be a daily trial. Following are some suggestions to use this book as more than a daily devotional reading:

1. Most of the entries end with a "challenge"—a way to walk out God's word by choosing joy and sharing joy with others. Try to embrace and implement these suggestions each day.

2. Many of the devotionals include a suggested worship experience. Take the time to type the URL into your computer or phone and listen to or maybe sing along with these songs.

3. Ask the Lord to bring other hymns or spiritual songs to mind that will remind you of the lesson learned and that minister to your spirit to bring you joy. Perhaps look up "joy" in the index of a hymnal.

4. Ask a friend (or relative—maybe a grandparent) to read with you. Perhaps determine how many to read each week and discuss them in person, on the phone, via Facetime, or by email. Staying connected to other believers will bring joy to both of you. With modern technology there is no excuse to be isolated.

5. Turn the book into a group study by delving into the cross references and context of the passages discussed in the book.

6. Use the book as a part of your family devotional time. If you don't have family devotional time, this could be a great place to start! Imagine leading your children to understand the Fruit of the Spirit.

CONTENTS

JEWELS ABOUT JOY FROM OTHERS

❖ "Joy is the soul of praise. To delight ourselves in God is most truly to extol him, even if we let no notes of song proceed from our lips. That God is, and that he is such a God, and our God, ours for ever and ever, should wake within us an unceasing and overflowing joy. To rejoice in temporal comforts is dangerous, to rejoice in self is foolish, to rejoice in sin is fatal, but to rejoice in God is heavenly. He who would have a double heaven must begin below to rejoice like those above."

Charles H. Spurgeon

From *The Treasury of David* as quoted at: https://biblehub.com/commentaries/psalms/33-1.htm

❖ "Joy is essential to the spiritual life. Whatever we may think of or say about God, when we are not joyful, our thoughts and words cannot bear fruit. Jesus reveals to us God's love so that his joy may become ours and that our joy may become complete. Joy is the experience of knowing that you are unconditionally loved and that nothing—sickness, failure, emotional distress, oppression, war, or even death—can take that love away. Joy is not the same as happiness. We can be unhappy about many things, but joy can still be there because it comes from the knowledge of God's love for us. . . . Joy does not simply happen to us. We have to choose joy and keep choosing it every day. It is a choice based on the knowledge that we belong to God and have found in God our refuge and our safety and that nothing, not even death, can take God away from us."

Henri Nouwen – found at: https://henrinouwen.org/meditations/joy/

❖ "Joy bursts in our lives when we go about doing the good at hand and not trying to manipulate things and times to achieve joy."

C.S. Lewis found at:
    https://bookroo.com/quotes/cs-lewis-quotes-about-joy

❖ "Even in the midst of unhappiness we can have joy—an inner peace that comes from knowing God loves us and is ultimately in control."

Billy Graham found at:
https://billygraham.org/answer/even-in-times-of-sorrow-joy-is-possible/

❖ "Joy is the appropriate emotional response to the unmerited and unlimited grace of God. Sometimes we need to ask ourselves, How can I not be joyful—when God made me with loving skill, when He became a Man in Bethlehem to identify with my needs, when He died to free me from my sins, when He rose to give me a bright future, and when He's coming back to take me to heaven? How can I not be joyful!"

David Jeremiah
Turning Points, December 2023, p. 18

JOY DEFINITIONS

H ere we are listing the basic definitions of the words used for joy, joyful, and rejoice in the Old and New Testaments. As with the "Love" introduction page, we have quoted these from *The Complete Word Study Dictionary: Old Testament*, Warren Baker and Eugene Carpenter, eds. and *The Complete Word Study Dictionary: New Testament*, Spiros Zodhiates, ed. Each entry continues on to show the different nuances of the words in specific verses. These books are an excellent resource. The numbering system corresponds to *Strong's Exhaustive Concordance of the Bible*.

HEBREW

H1523 gîyl – a verb meaning to rejoice.

H1524 gîyl – a masculine noun depicting rejoicing. It describes a happy state of affairs and actions compared to a previous state of suffering.

H2302 *châdâh* – A verb meaning to rejoice, to be glad. It depicts a joyous response to something or someone: the goodness of the Lord (Ex. 18:9); figuratively of a day of birth rejoicing (Job 3:6) in certain verb forms to indicate the Lord's making someone happy (Psalm 21:6-7)

H2304 *chedvâh* – a feminine noun denoting joy, gladness. The dwelling place of the Lord is the place of joy and gladness (1 Chr. 15:27). It specifically indicates the joy of the Lord which serves as the strength of the Israelites (Neh. 8:10).

H2305 *chedvâh* – An Aramaic feminine noun indicating joy, gladness. It denotes the Israelites attitude and response to the completing of the new temple in Ezra's day (Ezra 6:16).

H5102 *nâhar* - . . . II. A verb meaning to be radiant. It means to shine, to glow, to beam over deliverance from God (Psalm 34:5).

H5937 *'âlaz* – a verb meaning to rejoice, to exult, to be jubilant. It describes a state and act of celebration, approval, support for something; especially in exalting over God . . .

H5970 *'âlats* – a verb meaning to rejoice, to be jubilant. It is used of a person rejoicing, especially the Lord.

H6670 *tsâhal* – a verb meaning to cry out, to shout, to neigh. It refers to making a loud sound, usually of great delight and joy.

H7321 *rûwa'* - a verb meaning to shout, to sound a blast. The term occurs thirty-three times in the Old Testament and was utilized fundamentally to convey the action of shouting or the making of a loud noise . . . Many times the shout was a cry of joy, often in response to the Lord's creating or delivering activity on behalf of His people.

H7440 *rinnâh* – a feminine noun indicating glad shouting, joyful singing, crying out. It refers to the utterance and sound of a shout, a cry.

H7442 *rânan* – a verb meaning to shout for joy, to sing joyfully. It indicates the utterance or crying out of a person or persons. The character of the cry must be discerned by the context or actual intended use of the verb. Often it indicates crying out in joy, exaltation. It is used most often of exalting or praising the Lord.

H7445 *rᵉnânâh* – A feminine noun indicating a joyful shout, singing . . . It is used to indicate lips of joy. Lips that offer praise to God (Ps. 63:5).

H7797 *sûws* – a verb meaning to rejoice: to exalt; to be glad. It is a verb that indicates great rejoicing and jubilant celebration.

H8055 *sâmach* – a verb meaning to rejoice; to be joyful, to be glad; to gloat. It describes a state and agitation of rejoicing; of being happy . . .

H8056 *sâmêach* – An adjective meaning glad, happy, many, joyful. It means to be
filled with joy, to be exceedingly glad.

H8057 *simchâh* – a feminine noun meaning joy, rejoicing, gladness, pleasure. It refers to the reality, the experience and manifestation of joy and gladness. It refers to a celebration of something with joyful and cheerful activities . . . The Israelites were expected to worship and serve their God with joy (Deut. 28:47) . . . It refers to great celebration and joy at conquering one's enemy.

H8342 *sâsôwn* – a masculine noun indicating joy, gladness . . . in His own people at deliverance (Psalm 105:43) . . .God is the joy of His people (Isaiah 12:3).

H8643 *tᵉrûw'âh* – a feminine noun indicating a shout of joy; a shout of alarm, a battle cry. It refers to a loud, sharp shout or cry in general, but it often indicates a shout of joy or victory.

GREEK

G20 *agallíasis* - gen. agalliáseōs, fem. noun from agalliáō (21), to exult. Exultation, exuberant joy. Not found in Gr. writers but often meaning joy, exultation (Sept.: Ps. 30:5; 45:15; 65:12, rejoicing with song, dancing. See Ps. 126:2, 6); great joy (Ps. 45:7; 51:8, 12). In the NT, joy, gladness, rejoicing (Luke 1:14, 44; Acts 2:46; Heb. 1:9 from Ps. 45:7, oil of gladness with which guests were anointed at feasts, where used as an emblem of the highest honors [cf. Jude 1:24]).

G21 agalliáō; contracted agallió, fut. agalliásō, aor. ēgallíasa, from ágan (n.f.), much, and hállomai (242), to leap. To exult, leap for joy, to show one's joy by leaping and skipping denoting excessive or ecstatic joy and delight. Hence in the NT to rejoice, exult. Often spoken of rejoicing with song and dance (Sept.: Ps. 2:11; 20:5; 40:16; 68:3). Usually found in the mid. deponent agalliáomai. (I) Used in an absolute sense (Acts 2:26, "my tongue was glad," meaning I rejoiced in words, sang aloud; Luke 10:21; Acts 16:34)

(I)   Used in an absolute sense (Acts 2:26, "my tongue was glad," meaning I rejoiced in words, sang aloud; Luke 10:21; Acts 16:34). It is sometimes put after chaírō (5463), to rejoice, which is of less intense significance, and produces an expression meaning to rejoice exceedingly (Matt. 5:12; 1 Pet. 4:13; Rev. 19:7; see Ps. 40:16; 90:14).

G4640. *skirtáō*; contracted skirtó, fut. skirtésō. To leap, spring, especially of animals (Sept.: Mal. 4:2). To leap for joy, to exult (Luke 6:23). Of the fetus in the womb (Luke 1:41, 44 [cf. Sept. Gen. 25:22]).

G4796. *sugchaírō*; fut. sugcharó, 2d aor. sunechárēn, from sún (4862), together, and chaírō (5463), to rejoice. To rejoice together, to share in another's joy, with the dat. depending on sún (4862), together, in composition (Luke 1:58; 15:6, 9 [in these verses, the translation can be "to congratulate"]; 1 Cor. 12:26; 13:6; Phil. 2:17, 18; Sept.: Gen. 21:6, in the mid.).

G5463 *chaírō*; fut. charésomai or chairésō (Luke 1:14; John 16:20, 22; Phil. 1:18; Sept.: Hab. 1:15; Zech. 10:7), 2d aor. echárēn. To rejoice, be glad. Intrans.:

G5479 *chará* - fem. noun from chaírō (5463), to rejoice. Joy, rejoicing, gladness. . . "joy in the Holy Ghost," meaning the joy which the Holy Spirit imparts by His influence; 15:13; 2 Cor. 1:24; 2:3; 7:4, 13; 8:2; Gal. 5:22; Phil. 1:25; joy of faith, meaning in and arising from the faith of the gospel; 2:2, 29; 1 Thess. 1:6 [cf. Rom. 14:17]; 1 Thess. 3:9; 2 Tim. 1:4; Phile. 1:7; James 4:9; 1 Pet. 1:8; 1 John 1:4; 2 John 1:12)

ARAB SHEIK REJOICES OVER GOD'S MIRACULOUS DELIVERANCE OF HIS CHOSEN PEOPLE!!

And Jethro rejoiced[H2302] over all the good things the LORD had done for Israel, whom He had rescued from the hand of the Egyptians. Jethro declared, "Blessed be the LORD, who has delivered you from the hand of the Egyptians and of Pharaoh, and who has delivered the people from the hand of the Egyptians. Now I know that the LORD is greater than all other gods, for He did this when they treated Israel with arrogance."

Exodus 18:9-11

Jethro [Jĕth'rō]—pre-eminence or excellence. The father-in-law of Moses, and an Arab sheik and priest of Midian (Exod. 3:1, 4:18; 18:1-12). Called Reuel or Raguel meaning "friend of God" in Exodus 2:18 and Numbers 10:29, and Jether in Exodus 4:18. (1)

It is of particular interest that this priest was obviously a priest to Yahweh. In a sacrifice of thanksgiving, at which Aaron was present, Jethro performed the sacrifice and Aaron and the other elders came and ate bread and had fellowship with him (Ex. 18:12). (2)

The first person mentioned as having "rejoiced over all the good things the Lord has done for Israel" was not even a Jew. He was an Arab sheik and priest from Midian who worshipped the God of Abraham, Isaac, and Jacob. Jethro, apparently a Gentile, already believed in the one true God, but his belief was solidified and amplified when he heard all that Yahweh had done for His chosen people, the Israelites, in bringing them safely out of Egypt and miraculously destroying Pharoah's army. He had a joyous response to God's goodness and faithfulness to Moses and Israel. Later, this same Jethro gave Moses wise advice concerning the governing of so many people. The Lord used Moses's father-in-law to help Moses learn to delegate the judging of disputes among the tens of thousands of people as they traveled to the Holy Land.

What good thing has the Lord done for you? Have you rejoiced over it? On this side of Calvary, we have even more reason to rejoice. God sent His Son, Jesus, to live among men that we might understand the Father and then to die in our place on the cross. Even if you cannot think of an immediate "good thing" God has done for you, a lifetime could be spent rejoicing over Jesus saving us from sin and preparing us a place in paradise. Perhaps if we took time to recognize all the good things God has done for us, great and small, we would be able to rejoice more often.

Father, help us to recognize Your mighty hand at work on our behalf. Let us rejoice over triumphs, even small ones, that You allow us to experience. Let us rejoice that

You go before us in troubles and already have the answer to our problems just as You knew before Moses approached the Red Sea that You were going to part it for Your people to walk across on dry land.

CELEBRATE GOD'S PROVISION WITH JOY

For seven days you shall celebrate a feast to the LORD your God in the place He will choose, because the LORD your God will bless you in all your produce and in all the work of your hands, so that your joy[H8056] will be complete.

Deuteronomy 16:15: 16:13–17

The "Feast of Booths" (v. 13) is so called, because for a week they were to gather at the sanctuary and live in temporary structures. It begins on the fifteenth day of the seventh lunar month (modern September-October), at the end of the agricultural season after the grain was threshed and the grapes harvested. Naturally, the tithe of the harvest was to be brought at this feast, which was also to memorialize Israel's pilgrim experience in leaving Egypt (Lev. 23:43). In addition, this feast was to be a time of reading the law (31:10–13; Neh. 8). (3)

In Deuteronomy 16, Moses summarizes three major festivals: The Passover (Feast of Unleavened Bread), The Feast of Weeks (Pentecost), and The Feast of Tabernacles (Booths). The Feast of Tabernacles was a joyous occasion because they were celebrating the harvest of grain and grapes and praising God for His bountiful provision. The Israelites were also remembering their travel from Egypt to the Holy Land when they lived in tents because they were not yet in the home God had promised them. God took care of them in all their wilderness wanderings even though their journey was prolonged by forty years due to their lack of faith (Deuteronomy chapter 1). Their shoes and clothes did not wear out in forty years of travel!

> *Deuteronomy 29:5: For forty years I led you in the wilderness, yet your clothes and sandals did not wear out.*

In modern America, we have set aside only one day to celebrate all God has done for us, and we call it Thanksgiving. We definitely feast, but how many of us truly count our blessings from God and praise Him with joy on that day? Have you ever experienced God's provision in a miraculous way? We remember a time when after all the bills were paid for the month, we had about $12.00 left for groceries for the next three weeks. Talk about panic! However, God provided all we needed and then some through the generosity of our brothers and sisters in Christ. Reflect on the times that God has provided abundantly beyond your needs. Then "your joy will be complete." Perhaps if we took more time to contemplate God's provision and celebrate together with thanksgiving, we would have less stress and more joy!

Father, help us to remember that every good thing in our lives is a gift from You (James 1:17). Replace any fear or worry with the remembrance that You have always provided and will always provide for us. Take our cares and replace them with joy as we remember how You care for us (1 Peter 5:7).

DOES THE LORD REJOICE IN MY GOODNESS?

So the LORD your God will make you abound in all the work of your hands and in the fruit of your womb, the offspring of your livestock, and the produce of your land. Indeed, the LORD will again delight^H7797 in your goodness, as He delighted^H7797 in that of your fathers, if you obey the LORD your God by keeping His commandments and statutes that are written in this Book of the Law, and if you turn to Him with all your heart and with all your soul.

Deuteronomy 30:9-10

> H7797 - . . . It refers to the Lord's taking delight or joy over blessing, punishing, or disciplining His people if they need it (Deut. 28:63; 30:9; Jer. 32:41; Zeph. 3:7) (4)

In this passage, God is setting forth blessings and curses: His prescription for blessings to those who obey Him and a prescription for discipline for those who continue in disobedience. These particular verses describe God's delight or "rejoicing" in the KJV when Israel returns to obedience, and He restores them after a time of captivity. The Lord takes joy in blessing His children. He rejoiced when the nation of Israel walked in obedience. Although these promises are for His Chosen People, Israel, the Lord rejoices, also, over all who have received salvation by grace through faith in the Lord Jesus Christ of Gentiles (non-jews) as well as the Jews. His promise to provide abundantly for those who are obedient, still applies to those who trust in Christ today. Our salvation is completely by grace, and the price to redeem us was paid in full by Jesus on the cross. Nothing we do or fail to do can change our status as children of the Lord once we surrender our lives to Him and receive the gift of salvation. However, God still takes joy in His children when we are obedient to His will and His ways; and we will experience His blessing in our lives.

Are you walking in obedience to what you understand of God's word today? Does your life give God cause to rejoice? Is there anything that you need to change today by the power of the Holy Spirit within you in order to bring the Lord joy? Do you love the Lord God with all your heart and soul? These are good questions to ask ourselves periodically, not to be legalistic but out of desire to bring joy to the Father who loves us unconditionally and eternally. We are His joy simply because as our Father, He delights in us. But that joy is multiplied when we act on our desire to please our Heavenly Father by being obedient to His commands. We please the Lord the most by understanding that we are the children of the King and by behaving like children of the Most-High God.

Father, it is our desire to be pleasing to You, to know that You rejoice over our obedience. Please reveal to us anything in our lives that needs to change in order to be completely within Your will for us. Help us to recognize the Holy Spirit's nudges and correct any wrong behavior.

REJOICE IN OUR SUPREME SOURCE OF JOY

At that time Hannah prayed: "My heart rejoices[H5970] in the LORD in whom my horn is exalted. My mouth speaks boldly against my enemies, for I rejoice[H8055] in Your salvation.

1 Samuel 2:1

HANNAH'S SONG (2:1–10) The devotedness of Elkanah's wife and son stands out against the depravity of Eli's family. After giving her son to the Lord, Hannah poured out her heart in thanksgiving. Her words reveal an in-depth knowledge of God, His character, and His deeds. The prayer seems to rebuke Peninnah for the many spiteful things she had said to Hannah, but it prophetically goes beyond this domestic squabble to the triumph of Israel over her foes and to the eventual reign of Christ. Mary's song, often called the Magnificat (Luke 1:46–55), was obviously influenced by her knowledge of Hannah's song. (5)

My heart rejoiceth in the Lord (v. 1). The supreme source of Hannah's joy is not in the child but in the God who has answered her prayer. (6)

Hannah had prayed so fervently for a son that Eli the priest thought she was drunk! When she explained that she was barren and was praying God would open her womb, Eli told her God would answer her prayer. In her prayer, she vowed to dedicate her firstborn child to the Lord. At the end of 1 Samuel 1, she makes good on her promise and brings her young son Samuel to the house of God at Shiloh to serve with Eli the Priest. Then she bursts out in song, rejoicing in the Lord who answered her prayer. Her joy in the Lord could not be contained, and her rejoicing was jubilant. How could she give up her first and at that time, only child soon after he was weaned? How could she give up the child she had waited so long to bear? She did rejoice to have Samuel whose name means "God has heard" but rejoiced more in knowing the Lord who hears, cares, and answers prayers.

God does hear and answer our prayers, not always in the way we imagine but in the way that is best for us. We can rejoice that the Creator of the Universe knows our names, knows our needs, and knows our inmost thoughts. We can rejoice that this Almighty God sent His Son to die in our place and redeem us from the sin that would separate us from God. We can rejoice in the God of our salvation who has adopted us into His family. We can rejoice that God is our Father, and we are victorious because of His love. REJOICE!

Father, remind us that our joy is found in You and not in the things You give us. Help us to rejoice in our relationship with You as our loving Father rather than our judge.

REJOICE IN HIS PRESENCE

Now the people of Beth-shemesh were harvesting wheat in the valley, and when they looked up and saw the ark, they were overjoyed[H8055] at the sight.

1 Samuel 6:13

This verse needs a little backstory to be understood. The Israelites had taken the ark of the covenant into battle with them thinking that surely God would enable them to defeat the Philistines. However, God allowed the Philistines to not only triumph but to capture the ark and kill the priest Eli's two wayward sons. The ark symbolized God's presence with Israel. Therefore, this was a great loss felt by the entire nation. While the Philistines had the ark in their possession, God caused them great distress. First of all, the idol of their god Dagon fell over in the presence of the ark. They up-righted it, and the next day it not only fell over but its head and arms broke off! Then the Philistines were plagued by great, grotesque tumors and an infestation of rats. Finally, the leaders of their five cities asked their wise men how to send the ark back. According to their advice, the leaders placed a chest next to the ark containing five gold tumors and five gold rats as a guilt offering to Israel's God. They set the ark and the chest on a cart being pulled by two cows who had new calves and had never been yoked before. Then they penned the calves up so they couldn't follow. This way if the cows went in a straight line toward Israel instead of making a U-turn to take care of their calves, it must be God drawing them to Israel. You can imagine the shock and the joy the Israelite harvesters felt when they looked up to see the ark of the covenant that had been captured and gone for seven months suddenly arriving, being pulled by two cows! When the cows stopped, the people cut up the cart for firewood and sacrificed the cows to the Lord. The people rejoiced exuberantly to have the ark of God's presence back in Israel.

How much do we value the presence of the Lord? If you are His child, if you have surrendered your life to Jesus, His presence in the form of the Holy Spirit lives in you! No one can steal Him from you or you from Him (John 10:28-30). We no longer rely on a priest to atone for our sins before the holy of holies once a year. We no longer need to sacrifice animals to God. Jesus Christ became the perfect, sinless Lamb of God and died to atone for our sins. Because of our relationship with Jesus, the presence of God is with us at ALL TIMES! Have you rejoiced to be in His presence today?

Father, how humbling and awesome it is to realize You are with us at this very moment as we write this page! We rejoice that we have the privilege of knowing You as Savior, Lord, and Father. We rejoice that You hear our prayers and know our needs before we voice them. We rejoice to be continually in Your presence, personally and intimately. Help us to remember that truth daily.

At that time Hannah prayed: "My heart rejoices in the LORD in whom my horn is exalted. My mouth speaks boldly against my enemies, for I rejoice in Your salvation.

1 Samuel 2:1

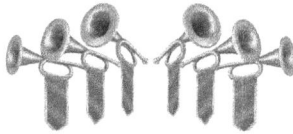

HANNAH REJOICED IN THE LORD

Hanna rejoiced more in knowing the Lord
who hears, cares, and answers prayers
than in the gift of a son He had given.
In song His greatness she declares.
Hannah was one of two wives
her husband Elkanah had married.
Peninnah was the other
and many children she carried.
Hannah, however, was barren.
No child was held in her arms.
Peninnah loved to taunt her
and cause her distress and alarm.
Peninnah had a problem with pride
thinking herself superior.
Hannah was humble and sweet
but was made to feel inferior.
Elkanah loved and comforted Hannah
always giving her a double portion

of the yearly sacrifice to the Lord
to dry her tears over her misfortune.

One year when they went to Shiloh
for the yearly worship of the Lord,
Hannah poured out her heart to God.
Her mouth moved but there were no words.
Eli the priest thought she was drunk
and rebuked her for indulging in wine,
but Hannah explained her spirit was oppressed;
and she bared her anguish to the Lord at that time.
Eli told her to go in peace and said,
"May the God of Israel grant your petition."
Hannah returned home with Elkanah
trusting in God's provision.
In her prayer, Hannah had vowed to God
to dedicate her son to His service.
When Samuel was born, she kept him home
until he was weaned to be nourished.
Then she took her young child
with her husband's permission
to serve with the priests
In humble submission.
Then she poured out a praise song
rejoicing in her Lord
who controls all the earth
by the sound of His word.

PRAISE FOR VICTORY BELONGS TO THE LORD

As the troops were returning home after David had killed the Philistine, the women came out of all the cities of Israel to meet King Saul with singing and dancing, with joyful[H8057] songs, and with tambourines and other instruments.

1 Samuel 18:6

Saul's men had been shaking in their sandals at the challenge of the Philistine's champion Goliath. The young man David had brought food for his brothers who served in the army. David did not fear Goliath because his trust was in the mightiness of his Lord and not in his own ability to fight. David went out in the strength of the Lord and killed the monstrous man, Goliath, using only a stone hurled from his sling. Then he chopped off the giant's head with Goliath's own gargantuan sword. This earned him the love and respect of King Saul's son Jonathan, and God knit their souls together like brothers for life. Jonathan made a covenant with David and presented him with items that effectively recognized him as taking Jonathan's place as the heir to the throne. Saul continued to send David into battle, and their victories over the Philistines continued to increase. Upon returning from one of these victorious campaigns, the women greeted King Saul with joyful dancing as they sang: "Saul has slain his thousands, and David his tens of thousands" (1 Samuel 18:7b). The women were celebrating the fact that God had given Israel the victory as they should have. However, because they attributed more glory to David than to him, Saul became extremely jealous of David. In reality, the praise, glory, and rejoicing belong to the Lord rather than any human instrument He used. When we forget that truth, we descend into a rabbit hole. If you know the rest of Saul's story, you know that his rabbit hole was jealousy and rage, and he did not finish well. David respected Saul's royalty and authority as God's chosen king and waited on the Lord to remove him from the throne even though Samuel had already anointed David as the next king of Israel.

The women were celebrating the victory over the Philistines with joyful singing, playing of instruments and dancing. They celebrated Saul and David, but the victory was ultimately the Lord's:

Proverbs 21:31: A horse is prepared for the day of battle, but victory is of the LORD.

Saul got caught up in jealousy instead of celebrating the fact that God had given both he and David the courage and skill to defeat the Philistines. How many times are we jealous of others' accomplishments instead of celebrating what the Lord is doing through them? If our focus is on God at work in others and ourselves instead of striving to be esteemed above others, we will work together in unity. We need to keep our eyes on and rejoice in what Jesus is doing rather than ranking others above or below ourselves.

Father, let our rejoicing be in what You are doing through Your people rather than feeling we have accomplished more than someone else. Let us celebrate all victories as gifts from You (James 1:17)! Let all praise and glory be ascribed to Your mighty name!

Maranatha Music reminds us that all glory for victory in our battles belongs to God. Listen to "The Battle Belongs to the Lord" here: https://www.youtube.com/watch?v=ir-XbtrgcRk

EXPLOSIVE SOUND OF REJOICING

Then Zadok the priest, Nathan the prophet, and Bena-iah son of Jehoiada, along with the Cherethites and Pe-lethites, went down and set Solomon on King David's mule, and they escorted him to Gihon. Zadok the priest took the horn of oil from the tabernacle and anointed Solomon. Then they blew the ram's horn, and all the people proclaimed, "Long live King Solomon!" All the people followed him, playing flutes and rejoicing[H8056] with such a great joy[H8057] that the earth was split by the sound. . . Zadok the priest and Nathan the prophet have anointed him king at Gihon, and they have gone up from there with rejoicing[H8056] that rings out in the city. That is the noise you hear.

1 Kings 1:38-40, 45

David's son Adonijah had presumptuously pro-claimed himself king of Israel while David lay on his deathbed. He falsely assumed David was now pow-erless. Nathan the prophet discovered this and had Bathsheba remind David of his vow to make Solomon his successor. David's body was failing, but his mind was still clear enough to exercise his authority to name his successor. He developed a plan to execute putting Solomon on the throne that would leave no doubt as to his chosen successor. David instructed Nathan, Zadok the priest, and Benaiah to put Solomon atop the king's mule, take him to Gihon, and anoint him as king. Zadok anointed Solomon as king then blew the ram's horn to announce the news. The people shouted, "Long live King Solomon". Their rejoicing and praise for God's provision of the new king was so loud it could be heard for miles. Meanwhile, Adonijah had been celebrating the fact that he usurped the throne when the party was interrupted by a clamorous noise. He was informed that the sound he heard was the rejoicing of the people over Solomon's coronation. Struck with fear of being executed by Solomon, Adonijah ran to the altar for sanctuary. Solomon graciously spared his life.

We find over and over that God's chosen people, the Israelites, celebrated with boisterous joy. Here they celebrated the Lord's provision of a new king to reign when David dies. Their joy is so unrestrained that the noise seems to "split the earth!" Clearly, the people recognized Solomon not only as David's choice of successor but God's choice as well. Have you ever experienced God working in your life to the point that your joy could not be contained? Do you long to see God move in such a way that people spontaneously burst out in celebration of Him? To be honest, I (Susie), often fear what people might think if I were extremely demonstrative in worship. I find myself holding back. Yet, as we study joy, I am finding that it is not only okay, but wonderful to fully express joy in the Lord! I (Susan) believe the Lord desires us to have the personal engagement of His presence through rejoicing in His goodness. Because we are created in God's image, we should be the embodiment of the Fruit of the Spirit, including effervescent joy.

Father, may we become more comfortable with expressing our joy in You. You are our Creator, Savior, Sustainer, AND the source of our joy. May our joy be complete in You and may our rejoicing overflow as a testimony to Your goodness!

REJOICING IN THE GOOD-NESS OF GOD

So at that time Solomon and all Israel with him—a great assembly of people from Lebo-hamath to the Brook of Egypt—kept the feast before the LORD our God for seven days and seven more days—fourteen days in all. On the fifteenth day Solomon sent the people away. So they blessed the king and went home, joyful[H8056] and glad in heart for all the good things that the LORD had done for His servant David and for His people Israel.

1 Kings 8:65-66

Solomon had completed building the Lord's Temple and had the Ark of the Covenant brought into the Temple to be placed in the Holy of Holies. He chose to celebrate this event at the time of the Feast of Tabernacles or Booths which celebrated not only the harvest but God's bringing His chosen people into the promised land. The nation celebrated not just the seven required days but an additional seven days, fourteen days in all.

To mark this great occasion with the dignity and solemnity it deserved, Solomon assembled all the elders of Israel with the tribal and family chiefs. As God's anointed shepherd, he involved all Israel through its elders and chiefs in the moving of the ark and the dedication of the temple. This involved more than mere pomp and ceremony. Solomon was serious about the spiri-

tual significance of this occasion; and he desired
that the heart of all Israel be knit together in the
dedication of the temple and, more important, in
the dedication of their hearts to God. (7)

The people went home joyfully but not just because it
was a great fourteen-day party. Their joy was found in
remembering all that God had done for their nation,
King David, and now King Solomon. They had just spent
time reflecting on God leading their forefathers to the
promised land by celebrating the Feast of Booths and
now also celebrated God's allowing Solomon to build a
great Temple to His glory and place the symbol of His
presence with them—the ark—in the Holy of Holies.
They went home celebrating the Source of their joy.
Have you ever gone on a retreat and been asked to just
reflect on the goodness of God for several days? How often do we remind ourselves of all the excellent things
God has done for us individually or as a local congregation? Journaling is a great way to reflect on God's power
in your life and have a record to refer back to when times
get tough. You can see God's faithfulness in the pages of
your journal.

*Father, we rejoice in the salvation You have gracious-
ly given us through Jesus. We rejoice in Your constant
provision for all our needs. We rejoice in the many answered prayers we've experienced. Lord, we will sing
of the goodness of God!*

Worship opportunity: Cece Winans singing "Goodness of God" https://www.youtube.com/watch?v=y81y-I01_3o8

JOY IN ADVANCE OF VICTORY

All these men of war, arrayed for battle, came to He-
bron fully determined to make David king over all Is-
rael. And all the rest of the Israelites were of one mind
to make David king. They spent three days there eating
and drinking with David, for their relatives had pro-
vided for them. And their neighbors from as far away
as Issachar, Zebulun, and Naphtali came bringing food
on donkeys, camels, mules, and oxen—abundant sup-
plies of flour, fig cakes and raisin cakes, wine and oil,
oxen and sheep. Indeed, there was joy^{H8057} in Israel.

1 Chronicles 12:38-40

Chapter 12 lists the mighty men and leaders who
came out to join David's army when he was exiled
from Saul's kingdom and staying at Hebron. It records
the fact that tens of thousands of men were unified in
supporting David as the future king of Israel.

> 12:38–40 The report of David's widespread sup-
> port closes with the observation that the people
> at Hebron, and the rest of the nation, were of "a
> single mind" in their support of David. They cel-
> ebrated their new king with joy and feasting. (8)

The people celebrated what we might call a "dinner on
the grounds of biblical proportions"—a fantastic feast
with provisions being donated from their kinsmen far
and wide. Food had to be brought in on beasts of burden

to provide for such a large army and the other people there celebrating the man God had chosen to be their new king. The Lord had brought together people from several of the tribes leading them to unite for the common cause of making David king. Saul is not yet defeated. David is not yet on the throne. Yet the people are celebrating with joy, trusting that God will make it come to pass.

The Bible tells us that we as Christians are victorious. We may not feel victorious in this moment, but we can rejoice in knowing that God will make us so. Whatever God has called us to do, He will enable us to complete. We will win the battles by the power of the Holy Spirit in us. As Paul wrote:

Romans 8:37-39 No, in all these things we are more than conquerors through Him who loved us. For I am convinced that neither death nor life, neither angels nor principalities, neither the present nor the future, nor any powers, neither height nor depth, nor anything else in all creation, will be able to separate us from the love of God that is in Christ Jesus our Lord.

We can celebrate with joy today even before seeing the completion of what God has called us to do because we trust in His ability to finish what He has started in us.

Philippians 1:6 (NLT) And I am certain that God, who began the good work within you, will continue his work until it is finally finished on the day when Christ Jesus returns.

Father, You may not have called us to join an army to support an earthly king, but You have called us to be Your army serving King Jesus. Help us to be faithful and to know we can rejoice in the victory over sin and death even now because You are our Commander, and You have never failed and will never fail!

Rejoice with CeCe Winans singing "Never Lost":
https://www.youtube.com/watch?v=bWli7nDX1FU

LIFT UP YOUR VOICE WITH JOY!

So the priests and Levites consecrated themselves to bring up the ark of the LORD, the God of Israel. And the Levites carried the ark of God on their shoulders with the poles, as Moses had commanded in accordance with the word of the LORD. David also told the leaders of the Levites to appoint their relatives as singers to lift up their voices with joy^{H8057}, accompanied by musical instruments—harps, lyres, and cymbals.

1 Chronicles 15:14-16

Two chapters earlier in 1 Chronicles 13, David had hastily attempted to bring the Ark of the Covenant up to Jerusalem so the Israelites could inquire of God, but because he did not do it in the proper order, disaster struck one of his men. Uzzah was one of two men accompanying the cart carrying the ark. When the oxen stumbled, he reached out and touched the ark to steady it. God struck him dead which may seem terribly harsh, but there were strict rules about the ark and how it was to be moved. Fast forward to chapter 15 which occurs three months later. David apparently has studied or inquired about how to transport the ark since Uzzah's death, and he makes sure everything is done according to what God told Moses. He prepared a tent to house the ark and enlisted the Levites to carry it according to the proper procedure. The Levites consecrated themselves in preparation for carrying the ark. David also asked them to appoint singers who would accompany the ark singing joyously and playing instruments. The word for joy in this context would indicate exuberant, exhilarating celebration! This was a high-octane worship event! They were to celebrate the symbol of God's presence being carried to the seat of David's kingdom, the capital of Israel.

In these verses, the ark is not yet placed in its new tabernacle in the City of David. However, even along the way, in eager anticipation of worshiping God together in Jerusalem, the Levites were already consecrating themselves and celebrating joyously. We do not usually join a procession into our worship center, but we should already be rejoicing in our Lord before we enter the doors. Before we even arrive at our local church building, we should prepare our hearts to worship the God of our salvation with thanksgiving.

Psalm 100:4 (VOICE) *Go through His gates, giving thanks; walk through His courts, giving praise. Offer Him your gratitude and praise His holy name.*

Father, You are so tremendous that words cannot express. Let Your joy flow through us so that others see Jesus in us so strongly they are attracted like moths to a flame. Let us worship You even as we travel through our week in preparation for celebrating You joyously together on Sunday.

OUR JOYOUS JOURNEY

We've embarked on a journey through the Bible,
studying the Fruit of the Spirit called joy.
We've found it to be an outward expression
of a feeling Satan cannot destroy.
God's people rejoice in deliverance
like allowing them to cross on dry land
by parting the waters of the Red Sea
then drowning Paroah's army, every man.
We've seen the Lord God rejoice
in the goodness of His chosen nation.
We've taken a look at what causes
our Heavenly Father's elation.
We've found the supreme Source of joy
is our Creator, Sustainer, Savior.
Joy, unlike temporary happiness,
is not dependent on others' behavior.
We find joy in the gifts God has given
as Hannah's son from Him was a present,
but we've found that true lasting joy
is found only in our Lord's presence.
We rejoice when we are victorious
because victory belongs to the Lord.
We can rejoice before the battle is won

because God remains true to His word.
We rejoice and we sing of God's goodness
cleansing us from sin so corrosive.
Our joy should be boisterous; indeed,
our rejoicing should be explosive.
So, lift up your voices with joy.
Sing and shout loudly in praise.
Rejoice in the Source of our Joy,
the One known as the Ancient of Days!

DANCE LIKE NO ONE
IS LOOKING

So David, the elders of Israel, and the commanders of thousands went with rejoicing[H8057] to bring the ark of the covenant of the LORD from the house of Obed-edom. . . As the ark of the covenant of the LORD was entering the City of David, Saul's daughter Michal looked down from a window and saw King David dancing and celebrating, and she despised him in her heart.

1 Chronicles 15:25, 29

As they carried the ark into Jerusalem, David and company continued to rejoice in the Lord. They were singing, playing instruments, and yes, even dancing in celebration of the Lord being present with them. David was wearing a simple linen tunic and ephod like the Levitical priests wore. He was dancing as he rejoiced in the Lord. However, his wife, Saul's daughter Michal looked out the window and was embarrassed to see her husband, the king, dancing in the street. In 2 Samuel 6:21-22a, David responds to her criticism of his being vulnerable in front of others: "But David said to Michal, "I was dancing before the LORD, who chose me over your father and all his house when He appointed me ruler over the LORD's people Israel. I will celebrate before the LORD, and I will humiliate and humble myself even more than this." David danced as if the only One watching was God! He is the only audience that truly matters. Worship to please the Audience of One.

This is not an excuse to be disorderly in our worship, but it is a reminder that our praise, our song, our exuberance is to please God and God alone. We are not performing for others' pleasure. We are not concerned with the criticism of those who worship differently than we do, nor should we be critical of them. Our worship is to please an audience of One. Some of us shout or sing loudly. Some worshipers jump up and down. Others are so deeply moved by the goodness of God they are completely consumed in silence for a time. If the Lord so moves you, sing like you're in the shower with no one else home, dance like no human is looking, breathe in His goodness silently. Whatever the Lord moves you to do in response to Him, just do it, taking no thought of anyone but God.

Father, let our worship of You be unrestrained by what we think others are thinking about us. Let us be so intently focused on You that the world around us fades from our thoughts and our hearts are completely Yours.

For your worship pleasure: Alan Jackson singing "Turn Your Eyes Upon Jesus. https://www.youtube.com/watch?v=4C31F00QEHQ

For those who are more boisterous, sing along with the Gaithers and friends on "The Joy of Heaven": https://www.youtube.com/watch?v=82J07Z2rLxg

WELCOME TO THE PARTY

Glory in His holy name; let the hearts of those who seek the LORD rejoice[H8055]. Splendor and majesty are before Him; strength and joy[H2304] fill His dwelling. Let the heavens be glad, and the earth rejoice[H1523]. Let them say among the nations, 'The LORD reigns!' Then the trees of the forest will sing for joy[H7442] before the LORD, for He is coming to judge the earth.

1 Chronicles 16:10, 27, 31, and 33 (see also Psalm 105:1-15)

H1523 *gîyl* - a primitive root; properly, to spin round (under the influence of any violent emotion), i.e. usually rejoice, or (as cringing) fear:—be glad, joy, be joyful, rejoice. (9)

David composed this Psalm glorifying the Lord after placing the ark of the covenant in its tabernacle in Jerusalem. Glory—brag on—God's name! Let those who have their focus on the Lord purposefully, lavishly, and extravagantly celebrate Him. If we desire to be strong, then we must seek, study, and find out what brings the Lord jubilation. What gives Him pleasure? If we are God's children and His most prized possession— His precious jewels—and if giving Him pleasure is our whole purpose in life, then His purpose will be to make us strong. Knowing that God is sovereignly powerful should surely give us the confidence that He can extend that strength to us, His beloved children. If the heav-

JOY: Blossoms among the Thorns

ens and the inhabitants thereof are jubilant over what God has done and is doing—if the very land is having a party—how much more should we who are living on the earth take part in the same? Let the sea exclaim and the fields raise exultations of the Lord. Then the trees of the earth make melody where they are planted. How much more should we make a joyful noise to the cadence of His praise?

When I was feeling blue and inadequate because of my physical limitations, the Lord made it clear to me that as far as He is concerned, the most accomplished athlete is no more favored than I am. We are on equal ground as far as the Lord's ability to glorify Himself though us. God gives me (Susan) the strength to choose to live joyfully for Him in the midst of my multitude of thorns (aka physical challenges). I am living proof of the reality of God's enablement to infuse joy into the ones He loves. God enables me (Susie) to overcome my thorn (clinical depression) in order to serve Him joyfully and share His joy with others. He gave me an incredible gift by bringing Susan into my life to inspire me to rise above the circumstances and rejoice in His goodness. As Paul wrote, God's strength is made perfect in humanity's weaknesses:

2 Corinthians 12:7b-10 So to keep me from becoming conceited, I was given a thorn in my flesh, a messenger of Satan, to torment me. Three times I pleaded with the Lord to take it away from me. But He said to me, "My grace is sufficient for you, for My power is perfected in weakness." Therefore I will boast all the more gladly in my weaknesses, so that the power of Christ may rest on me. That is why, for the sake of Christ, I delight in weaknesses, in insults, in hardships, in persecutions, in difficulties. For when I am weak, then I am strong.

It is His desire to perfect His strength and place His joy in all those who know Him intimately. God is giving you an invitation to the party celebrating His goodness. How will you R.S.V.P?

Father, fill us with joy overflowing so that the earth cannot outdo us in celebrating You!

REJOICING IN GENEROUS GIVING

And the people rejoiced[H8055] at the willing response of their leaders, for they had given to the LORD freely and wholeheartedly. And King David also rejoiced[H8055] greatly.

1 Chronicles 29:9

In 1 Chronicles 28, David explains that he had planned to build a great temple to house the ark of the covenant and be God's dwelling place on earth. However, the Lord told him he would not be allowed to build His house because he was a warrior who had shed blood. Instead, David's son Solomon, successor to the throne, would have the holy honor of building the temple in Jerusalem—God's house of prayer. David had the plan and had already begun amassing the materials knowing that Solomon was young and inexperienced. In 1 Chronicles 29:1-8, David assembles all the leaders of Israel and lists the amounts of gold, silver, precious stones, etc. that he has already set aside for building God's dwelling place. Then he asks them, "Now who will volunteer to consecrate himself to the LORD today?" (1 Chronicles 29:5b). The leaders proceed to donate generously and willingly toward the building of the temple. The people rejoiced that their leaders were giving so selflessly to create the temple as a place to honor, glorify, and worship the God of Israel—the one true God. David was jubilant as well to see that the people exuberantly supported his desire to build a house for the Lord.

In the last few years, we have had the privilege of donating toward renovations in our local place of worship. We rejoice in the ability to contribute and, also, rejoice in those who have the means to contribute more than we do. As a community of believers—the Messianic community—we need to rejoice anytime we see each other honoring God with our time, talents, and financial contributions. There are times God is leading us to improve a building both for safety and aesthetics. There are other times, God impresses us to direct more funds toward community service and missionary efforts. He may lead one person to donate in a different specific area than another person. We should rejoice in generous giving and not judge the giver as long as the intent is to honor God and obey Him. The Israelites were exceedingly glad that all the provisions for building the Lord's temple were being donated. They did not seem to be criticizing the use of all that wealth to honor God or second guessing the best way to spend that money. They were completely joyful that God's house would be sacred, spectacular, and splendid because it was to be the center of all Jewish worship.

Father, let our giving toward Your work be joyous and lavish. Help us to rejoice when others give willingly to further Your kingdom on earth. Give us wisdom to know where You would have us contribute both monetarily and with our time.

GOD LOVES JUBILENT, CELEBRATORY GIVERS

O LORD our God, from Your hand comes all this abundance[H1995] that we have provided to build You a house for Your holy Name, and all of it belongs to You. I know, my God, that You test[H974] the heart and delight in uprightness. All these things I have given willingly and with an upright heart, and now I have seen Your people who are present here giving joyfully[H8057] and willingly to You.

1 Chronicles 29:16-17

H1995 *hâmôwn* - . . . it also describes the roar of nature in the rain . . . In general usage, it also indicates wealth and a great supply or mass of things (1 Chr. 29:16; 2 Chr. 31:20; Jer. 49:32) (10)

D avid utters a prayer of thanksgiving and blessing over all the donations given to build God's Temple. God has rained down the blessing of great wealth for the nation of Israel, and David acknowledges that the items they had donated were truly originally God's gifts to them. He named one of the first and foremost principles of Christian stewardship: It all belongs to God. Sometimes our use of material goods is a proof test of our love for God.

H974 *bâchan* - a primitive root; to test (especially metals); generally and figuratively, to investigate:—

examine, prove, tempt, try (trial). (11) Strong's Exhaustive Concordance of the Bible

Zechariah 13:9b I will refine them like silver and test them like gold.

Prove is the word used in refining gold until it is so pure the refiner can see his/her own reflection in the molten metal like a mirror image. God works in our lives, testing and refining us, until we are conformed to and reflect the image of Jesus (Romans 8:29). He desires us to have a heart like His, to embody the character of Christ. David had wholeheartedly given out of his love for the Lord. The people of Israel had also given willfully and joyfully. The word for "joyfully" in the Hebrew means a joyful celebration.

In the New Testament, we read, "Each one should give what he has decided in his heart to give, not out of regret or compulsion. For God loves a cheerful giver" (2 Corinthians 9:7). The Israelites were joyful or cheerful givers. Think for a few minutes about your own giving. You may or may not believe Christians should tithe. Let's put that argument aside for the moment. When we decide in our heart to give a gift to God, the giving—whether it be a tithe or an offering other than a tenth—should be done cheerfully. Our giving should be a joyful celebration of the fact that God has provided everything we own and given us the privilege of giving back to Him. As Christians, our lives should be God's living conduits of cheerful giving, sharing God's goodness with others.

Father, thank You for providing not only for our needs but enough to share with others by giving back to You. Help us to remember the principle that everything belongs to You in the first place and not be reluctant to give back to You what is Yours in tithing or meeting specific needs You place on our hearts. May giving to You result in a happy dance!

SEEKING OUR SAVIOR: RADICALLY REJOICING IN RELATIONSHIP!!!

Now the Spirit of God came upon Azariah son of Oded. So he went out to meet Asa and said to him, "Listen to me, Asa and all Judah and Benjamin. The LORD is with you when you are with Him. If you seek[H1875] Him, He will be found by you, but if you forsake Him, He will forsake you . . ." Then they entered into a covenant to seek[H1875] the LORD, the God of their fathers, with all their heart and soul. And whoever would not seek[H1875] the LORD, the God of Israel, would be put to death, whether young or old, man or woman. They took an oath to the LORD with a loud voice, with shouting, trumpets, and rams' horns. And all Judah rejoiced[H8055] over the oath, for they had sworn it with all their heart. They had sought[H1245] Him earnestly, and He was found by them. So the LORD gave them rest on every side.

2 Chronicles 15:1-2, 12-15

H1875 *dârash* – Its most important theological meaning involves studying or inquiring into the Law of the Lord (Ezra 7:10) or inquiring of God. (12)

H1245 *bâqash* – It denotes seeking someone's presence, especially the Lord's. (13)

Azariah's prophecy boils down to: Seek God diligently and He'll let you find Him. Forsake Him for idols, and He will forsake you. He would hide Himself from them indefinitely. Therefore, King Asa led the Israelites to renew their covenant with the one true God and to seek Him wholeheartedly. As they did so, they also renewed their commitment to follow the Law by executing anyone who did not seek the Lord and followed false gods instead (Deuteronomy 17:2-5)! This stoning to death was only to be carried out upon the testimony of two or three witnesses, not just one. There could be no straddling the fence. One had to be all-in for God and not dipping into idol worship. The Israelites sought the Lord's presence and the understanding of His Law with all their heart (inmost thoughts) and soul (entire being). Upon renewing their covenant with God through this oath, they rejoiced to be in right relationship with their Creator.

We are blessed to live on this side of the cross, under the New Covenant of Christ's blood. Our salvation does not depend upon our ability to keep God's law because Jesus met the requirements of the Law and paid the price for our sin to delivered us from the wrath of God. What a cause for joy! However, God's word is still our guide for seeking God with our entire being. If we truly love the Lord, we will keep His commandments (John 14:15). How seriously do we take our obedience to the Lord? As we have seen, the Israelites knew obedience and seeking the Lord were serious matters, not to be taken lightly or flippantly. If we sincerely, diligently pursue a relationship with our God, He will enable us to know Him personally, deeply, and intimately. Perhaps we need to reevaluate how much time we spend truly seeking to enlarge not only our knowledge about God but our relationship with God.

Father, once we have surrendered to Jesus, our journey to seek You has only begun. Help us to spend time in Bible study, prayer, and meaningful fellowship with other believers to grow in our relationship with You, to know who You are instead of focusing only on what You can do for us.

Remember this: Whoever sows sparingly will also reap sparingly, and whoever sows generously will also reap generously. Each one should give what he has decided in his heart to give, not out of regret or compulsion. For God loves a cheerful^{G2431} giver. And God is able to make all grace abound to you, so that in all things, at all times, having all that you need, you will abound in every good work.

2 Corinthians 9:6-8

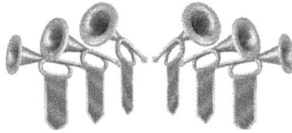

JOYFULLY GIVING
FROM WHAT GOD GAVE ME FIRST

Oh God, that I might decide in my heart
to give joyfully unto You
my works and deeds and material things
and continue faithful and true.
To give of the wealth You've given to me
knowing You will supply all my needs.
To not desire useless, covetous things
being thankful that in Christ I am free.
Oh God, I pray that You'll soften my heart
that I may be true to You.
Take my mind off my own concerns.
Help me do what You want me to do.

STAND FIRM AND REJOICE OVER GOD'S SAVING POWER

Then all the men of Judah and Jerusalem, with Jehoshaphat at their head, returned joyfully^{H8057} to Jerusalem, for the LORD had made them rejoice^{H8055} over their enemies. So they entered Jerusalem and went into the house of the LORD with harps, lyres, and trumpets.

2 Chronicles 20:27-28

The people of Ammon, Moab, and Mount Seir had formed a huge army to do battle against King Jehoshaphat and Judah. King Jehoshaphat called the people together to fast and pray and seek the Lord's help in the situation. They admitted to the Lord that they were powerless to battle this army on their own and needed His divine intervention. The Spirit of the Lord came upon a prophet named Jahaziel, and he assured Jehoshaphat and the people that God would fight for them. They just needed to show up for the battle and stand their ground. While the army of Judah marched toward the battlefield with the men in the lead singing, "Give thanks to the Lord, for His loving devotion endures forever" (2 Chronicles 20:21b), God created in-fighting among the attacking armies. They had turned on each other before the army of Jehoshaphat even got to the battlefield. "When the men of Judah came to a place overlooking the wilderness, they looked for the vast army, but there were only corpses lying on the ground; no one had escaped" (2 Chronicles 20:24). It took the men of Judah three days to pick up all the plunder! Therefore, King Jehoshaphat led the men of Judah and Jerusalem joyfully and triumphantly back into Jerusalem. They rejoiced over God's defeat of their enemies and heralded their entry into the city and God's temple with harps, lyres, and trumpets.

We've read accounts of the Lord intervening on behalf of Ukraine, trapping Russian tanks in mud, causing the invading troops to get lost, etc. The Lord still works mightily when His people seek Him with their whole hearts. We may not be fighting a physical, human army, but the Lord goes to battle against the principalities and powers of our enemy, Satan, on a regular basis. Once we have donned the armor of the Lord (Ephesians 6:10-18), Paul urges us to "stand firm." God furnishes us with His armor, but the battle still belongs to Him. Spiritual warfare can never be done in our own strength. We must always seek the Lord and go forth to face each day in the power of His might.

Father, as we put on the belt of truth, breastplate of righteousness, feet shod with the gospel, the shield of faith, and the helmet of salvation carrying the sword of the Spirit which is the word of God in our hearts, help us to bathe each day in prayer seeking You and trusting You to fight our battles and lay out the enemy before we even reach the battlefield.

REJOICING OVER RIGHTFUL HEIR MADE KING

When Athaliah heard the noise of the people running and cheering the king, she went out to them in the house of the LORD. And she looked out and saw the king standing by his pillar at the entrance. The officers and trumpeters were beside the king, and all the people of the land were rejoicing[H8056] and blowing trumpets, while the singers with musical instruments were leading the praises. Then Athaliah tore her clothes and screamed, "Treason, treason!" . . .

Moreover, Jehoiada put the oversight of the house of the LORD into the hands of the Levitical priests, whom David had appointed over the house of the LORD, to offer burnt offerings to the LORD as is written in the Law of Moses, with rejoicing[H8057] and song, as ordained by David. He stationed gatekeepers at the gates of the house of the LORD, so that nothing unclean could enter for any reason. He also took with him the commanders of hundreds, the nobles, the rulers of the people, and all the people of the land, and they brought the king down from the house of the LORD and entered the royal palace through the Upper Gate. They seated King Joash on the royal throne, and all the people of the land rejoiced[H8055]. And the city was quiet, because Athaliah had been put to the sword.

2 Chronicles 23:12-13, 18-21

Athaliah was—in modern lingo—a piece of work! When her son King Ahaziah was killed by Jehu, she proceeded to annihilate all his heirs—her grandsons! Athaliah's greed for power superseded any maternal or grandmotherly instinct she may have had. However, "Because Jehoshabeath, the daughter of King Jehoram and the wife of Jehoiada the priest, was Ahaziah's sister, she hid Joash from Athaliah so that she could not kill him" (2 Chronicles 22:11b). He must have been about a year old when his aunt hid him and his nurse. They stayed in hiding for six years. In 2 Chronicles 23, Joash is seven years old; and Jehoiada the priest decides it is time for him to assume his rightful, royal place on his father's throne as he was a descendant of David. Jehoiada wisely surrounded the young king with armed Levites inside the Temple. When his grandmother—the wicked Athaliah who had used objects from God's Temple in the worship of Baal and further desecrated the Lord's house —heard the commotion of the people rejoicing and saw King Joash standing by a pillar in the temple, she tore her robes and had the audacity to call it treason! Jehoiada had her escorted outside the temple and put to death not only because she had usurped the throne by murdering the heirs but because she had worshipped Baal and led the people to worship false gods as well. When King Joash was officially anointed, crowned, and seated on the throne, "all the people of the land rejoiced."

The people rejoiced to see the rightful heir become king and the Levites and priests worshiping in the Temple as they should. They rejoiced to see good triumph over evil. God's plan is always the right plan, and He had ordained that David's descendants should rule. Jehoiada understood that he must be sure the rightful heir was crowned king. Jesus is the final King in the line of David. We should rejoice to see His kingdom grow. We can rejoice right now even when difficulties and trials come because we know the ultimate end of history which is HIS-story. We can rejoice that He has made us witnesses to the truth that He is the King of kings. We rejoice because His Holy Spirit lives in us, "Christ in you, the hope of glory" (Colossians 1:27b)

Father, remind us to rejoice in the fact that Jesus is already crowned King and seated at Your right hand. Here on earth, Jesus was crowned with thorns, but we know when He comes again, He will be crowned with glory!

CHEERFULLY CELEBRATING THE OPPORTUNITY TO CONTRIBUTE

At the king's command a chest was made and placed outside, at the gate of the house of the LORD. And a proclamation was issued in Judah and Jerusalem that they were to bring to the LORD the tax imposed by Moses the servant of God on Israel in the wilderness. All the officers and all the people rejoiced[H8055] and brought their contributions, and they dropped them in the chest until it was full.

2 Chronicles 24:8-10

Joash who became King of Judah when he was only seven years old, ruled wisely and rightly under the guidance of Jehoiada the priest. When he was a little older, he decided to repair the temple and replace the sacred objects that Athaliah's sons had used in the worship of the Baals. He told the Levites to go out and collect the temple taxes from all the people as prescribed in the Law given to Moses. However, it appears that the Levites were lazy as his command was not carried out. Therefore, he placed a chest outside the Temple gate and issued a proclamation for the people of Judah and Jerusalem to bring their temple taxes and place them in the chest. The Levites had failed to go to the people to collect the tax, but the people willingly traveled to Jerusalem to pay it. In fact, they rejoiced at the opportunity to contribute to restoring the Temple of the Lord. People kept bringing their contributions until the chest was filled numerous times.

Do we rejoice to give to our local church? We are not charged a tax that is collected and enforced. Our offerings are of our own free will as the Lord has impressed upon us what to give. Some of us believe in tithing—giving a tenth of our income—each time we are paid. If so, do we do this grudgingly or with joy? Many times, our local congregation is asked to pray about giving above what we normally do in order to repair our building, buy new items used in our worship service, etc. Do we grumble about this, or do we earnestly seek the Lord in deciding an amount to donate? Do we celebrate that God includes us in supporting the ministry of our local church? Are we remembering that first principle of giving, the fact that it all belongs to God?

Father, we rejoice that You have enabled us to tithe and often to give offerings beyond our tithe. We thank You for supplying all our needs and showing us creative ways to give to our local church and other ministries. Help us to always take joy in giving back to You!

JOYFULLY JOIN IN WORSHIPING OUR LORD

When the offerings were completed, the king and all those present with him bowed down and worshipped. Then King Hezekiah and his officials ordered the Levites to sing praises to the LORD in the words of David and of Asaph the seer. So they sang praises with gladness[H8057] and bowed their heads and worshiped.

2 Chronicles 29:29-30

King Hezekiah's predecessor, King Ahaz, had not sought the Lord or obeyed Him. He had allowed unclean things to be brought into the Temple and had even closed its doors. Temple worship ceased during the reign of King Ahaz. King Ahaz was so evil he even sacrificed some of his children in the fire as offerings to false gods. By the grace of God, King Ahaz's son Hezekiah "did what was right in the eyes of the LORD, just as his father David had done" (2 Chronicles 29:2). King Hezekiah commanded the Levites to consecrate themselves and cleanse the temple of any impure items. He burned those things in the valley of Kidron. Once the temple and the articles needed for worship were cleansed, King Hezekiah had animals brought to the temple to be offered as a sacrifice and sin offering to the Lord. As the offerings were being burnt the Levites played instruments and sang in worship of the Lord. After the offerings, praises—particularly psalms of David and Asaph—continued to be sung with joy as they worshiped the one true God. The people had not celebrated and worshiped God during the reign of Ahaz which lasted sixteen years. Therefore, they rejoiced greatly to be able to reinstate temple worship. They were way overdue for the freedom and ability to praise the Lord exuberantly in His House of Prayer.

During the pandemic the last few years (2020-2023), many churches temporarily closed in order to stop the spread of the Covid-19 virus. Then they re-opened with "social distancing" and wearing masks. Because Susan is immune-compromised due to her cerebral palsy and weaker lungs, we have not been able to return to church. We participated in small group study via Zoom and watched the worship service via live streaming. A few months ago, I (Susie) attended worship because I felt a pressing need to ask the congregation to pray for me by going to the altar during prayer time. When I walked into the foyer, several friends came up to hug me. I became overwhelmed and burst into tears. I was starved for the in person "familyship" of corporate worship. I rejoiced as I sang the praise songs through tears. It is heart-wrenching for Susan to not be able to go to church in person because the church is her home in so many ways. Susan is working to get reacclimated to sitting in her power chair long enough to go to church. We will have a fantastic, joyous celebration when we are both able to attend worship services in person! This Sunday, if you are able to attend worship at your local church, REJOICE!!!

Father, we thank You that the leaders of North Pointe Baptist have worked hard to include us in worship throughout this pandemic. We praise you for a pastor and other church members who have brought "family-ship" into our home when we could not come to them. We rejoice to be able to worship You together even in our apartment.

P.S. Please pray for more volunteers to help transfer Susan in and out of her chair to enable her to build up stamina to be in the chair for both small group and worship service on Sundays. Pray for pain relief that does not reduce her cognitive abilities.

TEMPLE WORSHIP RESTORED: PEOPLE PRAISE THE LORD

Hezekiah said to the crowd, "Now that you are once again acceptable to the LORD, bring sacrifices and offerings to give him thanks" . . .

Furthermore, the burnt offerings were abundant, along with the fat of the peace offerings and the drink offerings for the burnt offerings. So the service of the house of the LORD was established. Then Hezekiah and all the people rejoiced[H8055] at what God had prepared for the people, because everything had been accomplished so quickly.

2 Chronicles 29:31, 35-36

Hezekiah had made sure the temple was spic and span, ceremonially cleansed, and refurbished. The Levites accomplished this massive makeover in only sixteen days. Now that the place was once again prepared for praising and worshiping the Lord, Hezekiah told the people to bring sacrifices to thank the Lord. God once again provided everything that was needed to properly worship Him. The people were able to bring 70 bulls, 100 rams, and 200 lambs as sacrifices to please the Lord. Then they brought an additional 600 bulls and 3,000 sheep to sacrifice in asking the Lord to bless them. Not all the priests were ceremonially prepared to offer sacrifices, but the Levites had consecrated themselves and pitched in to skin all those beasts. King Hezekiah had successfully brought back the temple worship his father had neglected. The people celebrated joyously because God had enabled everything to be prepared in such a short time and blessed them with an abundance of animals to offer for sacrifice.

Notice that the people were not patting themselves on the back for bringing all the animals for sacrifice. The Levites and priests were not complimenting themselves on the speedy cleansing of the Temple. King Hezekiah was not strutting about taking credit for reestablishing worship in the Temple of the Lord in Jerusalem. No, they were rejoicing in all that God had done through them, but the glory and credit was given to the Lord. Are we remembering that first principle of stewardship? Everything we "own" really belongs to the Lord who allows us to use it. May it bring us joy to be able to return to Him a portion of the blessings He has given us. We rejoice, not in our own ability to bring a large offering, but in God's ability to lead us in using what He has provided to further His kingdom on earth. As you put your offering in the plate or give it online, rejoice that the Lord is allowing you to be a part of His work here on the Earth while storing up treasure in Heaven (Matthew 6:20).

Father, we rejoice because You are allowing us to be Your vessels to overflow with blessings for others. Thank You for providing more than enough for us to worship You by giving back a portion of what You have given us.

Then the LORD said to Moses, "Speak to the Israelites and say to them, 'These are My appointed feasts, the feasts of the LORD that you are to proclaim as sacred assemblies."

Leviticus 23:1-2

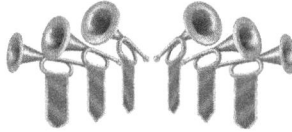

JOYOUS FESTIVITIES

As Moses had instructed God's people in the wilderness,
the Israelites celebrated feasts throughout the year.
There were seven feasts or sacred assemblies
that were solemn occasions celebrated with cheer.
The Passover feast reminded God's people
death passed over homes with blood on the door posts.
As Christians, Christ was our final Passover Lamb
who satisfied the wrath of the Lord of Hosts.
By His death on the cross and His resurrection,
Jesus conquered death and defeated the grave.
The Passover foreshadowed our Lord's victory,
and we celebrate that from death we are saved.

For the seven days of the Feast of Unleavened bread
the Israelites ate nothing containing yeast.
This reminded them of their haste in fleeing Egypt
though it might not sound like a tasty feast.
The Jews cleansed their houses of any and all leaven,
In the New Testament we find it represented sin.

Those of us who have trusted Jesus as Savior
must repent and ask Him to cleanse us within.

The Feast of First Fruits was to celebrate dependance
on the Lord who provided for all of their needs,
who delivered them from Egypt to the Promised Land
where abundance of grain grew from their seeds.
Jesus is the "first fruits of those who have fallen asleep"
referring to His resurrection from the dead.
Christ was the first to receive a glorified body.
We will be glorified like Him from our toes to our head!

The Feast of Weeks we now know as Pentecost
celebrated harvest, God's promised provision for their
needs.
The first Pentecost after Jesus's resurrection,
the promised Helper from Jesus was received.
The Holy Spirit came to dwell in believers
to empower and comfort them all of their days.
As we go about the work to harvest men's souls,
the Holy Spirit directs us in God's will and ways.

The Feast of Trumpets called Rosh Hashanah
was the beginning of the Jewish New Year.
The blast of the shofar and blowing of trumpets
let them know the Day of Atonement was near.
The next ten days were called "the days of Awe"—
a solemn time of reflection and repentance.
Burnt offerings and grain offerings were made
and awe of Almighty God filled those in attendance.

When Jesus returns to this earth the next time
it will be with the sound of trumpets
to call all those who trust in Christ to rise
and the earth to prepare for judgment.

The Day of Atonement—Yom Kippur—
was the holiest of all Holy Days.
The blood of a goat atoned for their sins.
A goat released symbolized taking sins away.
The intricate ceremony conducted by the priest
symbolized God's forgiveness of sins for one year.
There was much introspection and confession
as the Day of Atonement drew near.
When Jesus sacrificed Himself as our Passover Lamb,
He provided atonement for all who trust in Him.
A priest no longer needs to offer sacrifices yearly.
Jesus atoned for and removed our sin
bringing that to an end.
Jesus is the only High Priest we need
who as He died on the cross said, "It is finished."
This final sacrifice was completely sufficient,
and its effectiveness cannot be diminished.

The Feast of Tabernacles or Feast of Booths,
also called Sukkot was a joyous celebration.
The autumn harvest had been brought in,
God continued to provide for His chosen nation.
During the eight days of sacrificing and feasting
the people lived in tabernacles or booths
to remind them of the journey to the promised land,

that God's provision and protection was truth.
The Gospel of John says Jesus "tabernacled" with us
when He lived on earth in bodily form.
The Feast of Tabernacles looks forward to the time
Christ will live among us on earth once more.
Until that time God provides for and protects
those who await the returning of their Lord.
As we live in the wilderness of this fallen world,
we rejoice in the promises found in His word.

CELEBRATE!
THE FINAL PASSOVER LAMB
HAS RISEN FROM THE GRAVE!

The Israelites who were present in Jerusalem celebrated the Feast of Unleavened Bread for seven days with great joy[H8057], and the Levites and priests praised the LORD day after day, accompanied by loud instruments of praise to the LORD. And Hezekiah encouraged all the Levites who performed skillfully before the LORD. For seven days they ate their assigned portion, sacrificing fellowship offerings and giving thanks to the LORD, the God of their fathers. The whole assembly agreed to observe seven more days, so they observed seven days with joy.

2 Chronicles 30:21-23

The Passover Feast and Feast of Unleavened Bread which begins the next day had not been celebrated at the prescribed time—the 14th day of the first month—because the Temple had not been made ready and the people were not consecrated and prepared to participate. The Passover feast celebrated that the angel of death passed over the houses marked by the blood of the sacrificial lamb but killed all the firstborn children and animals of the people of Egypt. The next day, the Israelites left in haste and did not make bread containing yeast that would have to rise which God called the bread of affliction (Deuteronomy 16:3). Leavening (such as yeast) represents sin, so all leaven was cleansed from their houses and only flat bread without leaven was eaten for the seven days of the feast. They remembered this salvation of their forefathers and the fact that God brought them out of Egypt joyfully each year with the Passover and Feast of Unleavened Bread. Since they had failed to celebrate at the proper time, King Hezekiah issued a decree that Passover would be celebrated on the 14th day of the second month. He invited people from tribes other than Judah saying God might help the ones from their tribes who had been taken captive by Assyria. Many of those people scorned the invitation, but some came to Jerusalem to join the celebration. All the people who had gathered in Jerusalem celebrated for seven days "with great joy!" The Levites and priests sang praises and played loud instruments throughout the festival. The Passover was a time for rejoicing in the salvation the Lord provided for the nation of Israel.

Jesus Christ was the final, perfect Passover Lamb. The One of whom John the Baptist said, "Behold, the Lamb of God who takes away the sin of the world!" (John 1:29 NASB), was sacrificed on the cross to cover our sin and grant us eternal life. Jesus is our Passover! Do we celebrate our deliverance from sin with great joy? When we celebrate what the world now calls "Easter" by remembering the death and resurrection of Jesus, do we rejoice that this final Passover Lamb delivered us from bondage to sin and insured our entrance into the ultimate Promised Land? Perhaps we should instigate a 7-day celebration of the resurrection of our Lord!

Father, we rejoice in the deliverance You provided for us by sending Your only begotten Son to the cross to die as our Passover Lamb. When the cares of this world try to drag us down, help us to remember the joy of our salvation! Let the celebration begin!

"MORE, MORE, MORE!" CRIED THE WORSHIPERS

The whole assembly agreed to observe seven more days, so they observed seven days with joy[H8057]. For Hezekiah king of Judah contributed a thousand bulls and seven thousand sheep for the assembly, and the officials contributed a thousand bulls and ten thousand sheep for the assembly, and a great number of priests consecrated themselves. Then the whole assembly of Judah rejoiced[H8055] along with the priests and Levites and the whole assembly that had come from Israel, including the foreigners who had come from Israel and those who lived in Judah. So there was great rejoicing[H8057] in Jerusalem, for nothing like this had happened there since the days of Solomon son of David king of Israel. Then the priests and the Levites stood to bless the people, and God heard their voice, and their prayer came into His holy dwelling place in heaven.

2 Chronicles 30:23-27

King Hezekiah and all the people could not get enough of celebrating. Therefore, Hezekiah and all the officials donated more animals to be sacrificed to the Lord and enjoyed by the people. The worshipers felt the energy and vitality of participation in holy activity that the priests enjoyed on a regular basis. Those who were not professional worshipers wanted to continue soaking in God's presence. Their joyous celebration resounded throughout Jerusalem for another seven days. The only other time a feast extended to another week prior to this had been when Solomon dedicated the Temple. The priests and Levites blessed the people and "God heard their voice, and their prayer came into His holy dwelling place in heaven" (2 Chronicles 30:27b). God inhabits, abides, is enthroned upon the praises of His people Israel (Psalm 22:3). The people worshiped, praised, and rejoiced in God, and He honored the Levites prayer to bless them.

Have you ever participated in a worship service that continued past the usual time to end it, and no one was upset or looking at their watches or phones? Have you ever been so caught up in praising God and rejoicing in the way He was moving in people that you didn't want the service to end? We both have experienced that kind of moving of the Holy Spirit and long to see it again. Are you willing to set aside the time constraints we usually impose on ourselves and just pray, "More, more, more! Holy Spirit, You are welcome to keep moving in our hearts. We are filled with joy to see Your handiwork and pray it would overflow to the entire 'familyship'!"?

Father, we rejoice in how You are working in our local congregation. Lord, we long to see revival among Your children. We pray You would bring a Great Awakening to our country, and we would see many people turn to You and trust Jesus as their Savior and Lord.

GOD RECONSTRUCTS HIS TEMPLE IN YOU

But many of the older priests, Levites, and family heads who had seen the first temple wept loudly when they saw the foundation of this temple. Still, many others shouted joyfully[H8057]. The people could not distinguish the shouts of joy[H8057] from the sound of weeping, because the people were making so much noise. And the sound was heard from afar. Then the people of Israel— the priests, the Levites, and the rest of the exiles—celebrated the dedication of the house of God with joy[H2305]. For seven days they kept the Feast of Unleavened Bread with joy[H8057], because the LORD had made them joyful[H8055] and turned the heart of the king of Assyria toward them to strengthen their hands in the work on the house of the God of Israel.

Ezra 3:12-13, 6:16, 22

3:12 the first temple. The temple built by Solomon (cf. 1 Kin. 5–7). wept with a loud voice. The first temple had been destroyed 50 years earlier. The old men, who would have been about 60 years or older, knew that this second temple did not begin to match the splendor of Solomon's temple nor did the presence of God reside within it (cf. Hag. 2:1–4; Zech. 4:9, 10). The nation was small and weak, the temple smaller and less beautiful by far. There were no riches as in David and Solomon's days. The ark was gone. But most disappointing was the absence of God's Shekinah glory. Thus the weeping. shouted . . . for joy. For those who did not have a point of comparison, this was a great moment. Possibly Ps. 126 was written and sung for this occasion. (14)

The shouts of joy reverberated; there was a joyous echo throughout the city. God's temple was being rebuilt. The Lord filled the people continuously with jubilation and praise. God is the reservoir from which the believer draws joy. The people of Israel were ecstatic to be back home from captivity in Babylon and excited to be free once again. They were elated to dedicate the revitalized temple for God's purposes. Let us remember that we ourselves are God's temple where He abides. We can worship wherever we are. Worship does not reside in a building of brick and mortar. God has made us living temples—His abiding place—via the Holy Spirit. Jesus said, "I am the vine and you are the branches. The one who remains in Me, and I in him, will bear much fruit. For apart from Me you can do nothing" (John 15:5).

When I (Susan) was feeling excluded and isolated, I prayed. The Lord revealed to me that He feels the frailty of loneliness exponentially on behalf of all His children. In Jesus's humanness, He felt loneliness as the disciples failed to pray in the garden and rejection on the cross as the Father turned His face away. Shocker: Jesus felt loneliness! We no longer need to feel lonely because our joy is fulfilled as we take up our abode in Christ, and the

Holy Spirit makes us His dwelling place—His temple (1 Corinthians 3:16). The antidote to loneliness is knowing that ". . . in Him we live and move and have our being" (Acts 17:28). Has Christ restored your building to be His temple? If not, surrender yourself to His reconstruction of your life today!

Father, we are Your dwelling place. We are never alone. We can worship You even in the quietness of our own home because You are present with us and in us. What an awesome reality! Thank You for filling us with the joy of Your presence.

THE JOY OF THE LORD

Then Nehemiah told them, "Go and eat what is rich, drink what is sweet, and send out portions to those who have nothing prepared, since today is holy to our Lord. Do not grieve, for the joy[H2304] of the LORD is your strength."

Nehemiah 8:10

8:10–12 the joy of the LORD is your strength. The event called for a holy day of worship to prepare them for the hard days ahead (cf. 12:43), so they were encouraged to rejoice. The words they had heard did remind them that God punishes sin, but also that God blesses obedience. That was reason to celebrate. They had not been utterly destroyed as a nation, in spite of their sin, and were, by God's grace, on the brink of a new beginning. That called for celebration. (15)

The people of Israel had abandoned giving their affection to their first Love and had even worshiped false gods. They had prostituted themselves to other things and matters instead of worshiping the one true God. They were feeling guilty because they had placed people, things, and idols above God. They had returned from captivity and were seeking the Lord and His forgiveness for their iniquities. They needed restoration and reunification. Ezra read from the Book of the Law continuously all morning, and the people attentively and reverently listened. As they were hearing him read, the weight of everything they had done that was against the Law of the Lord became painfully clear, and they wept. Nehemiah encouraged them to focus on the fact that they had come back to being instructed and had returned to their first Love and sustenance. He told them not to be completely downcast or utterly depressed. Their jubilation would come from bringing pleasure to the Lord and would empower them to walk in divine purposes. What brings pleasure or joy to God? Our obedience to His will and ways.

It takes divine power and conviction every morning for me (Susan) to get up, being "bed-found." I have altered the more common term "bed-bound" because it sounds so negative, as if I were shackled to the bed! I much prefer "bed-found" because my bed is where you will find me much of the time. Because of who God is in me, I have influence outside these four walls even though, for the moment, I am within this room most of the time. As far as God is concerned, these four walls do not define me, nor do they confine me. This 942-square-foot apartment could only confine me if I didn't choose to obey the purpose God designed for me. My obedience to seek Him first and share His love and grace with others brings God joy and, in turn, His blessing to me. My joy is found in bringing joy to my Lord.

God created you to be YOU specifically. Have you sought the Lord about your own purpose? Are you walking in that purpose daily to bring joy to the Lord and thus to yourself? As Jerry Bridges wrote in The Fruitful Life:

> It is both our privilege and our duty to be joyful. To be joyless is to dishonor God and to deny His love and His control over our lives. It is practical atheism. To be joyful is to experience the power of the Holy Spirit within us and to say to a watching world, "Our God reigns". (16)

Father, help us to draw strength from pleasing You. Infuse us with the power needed to fulfill Your purposes for us. Let us find our joy in worshiping and obeying You.

JOY OF JERUSALEM HEARD FROM AFAR!

At the dedication of the wall of Jerusalem, the Levites were sought out from all their homes and brought to Jerusalem to celebrate the joyous[H8057] dedication with thanksgiving and singing, accompanied by cymbals, harps, and lyres . . . On that day they offered great sacrifices, Rejoicing[H8055] because God had given them great joy[H8057]. The women and children also rejoiced[H8055], so that the joy[H8057] of Jerusalem was heard from afar. And on that same day men were appointed over the rooms that housed the supplies, contributions, firstfruits, and tithes. The portions specified by the Law for the priests and Levites were gathered into these storerooms from the fields of the villages, because Judah rejoiced[H8057] over the priests and Levites who were serving.

Nehemiah 12:27, 43-44

There was a resounding, rippling, reverberating sound of joy throughout Jerusalem that could be heard from afar! Why this exuberant celebration? Word had come to Nehemiah in Susa where he served as a cup bearer to King Artaxerxes of Persia, that the walls of Jerusalem were broken down and the gates burned down as well. He wept, fasted, and prayed for his homeland then courageously approached the king for leave to go repair the walls (Neh. 2). God answered his prayer, and he was given permission and safe passage to return to Jerusalem. God enabled Nehemiah to unify the people and lead them in rebuilding the city wall in only 52 days even with attacks from their enemies. Men carried building materials and tools in one hand and swords or spears in the other. Nehemiah records that "the people had a mind to work" (Nehemiah 4:6b), and the Lord helped them achieve this fantastic feat. When the wall was complete, all the Levites were summoned from their homes. Nehemiah divided the singers into two groups, each walking a different direction around the wall so that the joyful sound echoed across Jerusalem. The remnant of God's people had sought the Lord and returned from exile. Under Ezra's leadership, God's temple was restored. Now, under the direction of Nehemiah the walls surrounding Jerusalem were once again a strong fortress against their enemies. Nehemiah had prayed fervently for his nation, and God had mightily answered His prayer. Therefore, the sound of rejoicing was heard far and wide!

Nehemiah wept, fasted, and prayed for days, interceding on behalf of his nation. Our nation has strayed greatly from our Judeo-Christian heritage. We rant about blatant sin. We post memes about the state of our government. We may even participate in civil protests. But how many of us weep, fast, and pray for America? How many of us intercede fervently for our national leaders? Perhaps less standing up to complain and more kneeling to humbly seek the Lord and repent of our sin and that of our country is in order.

Father, we ask Your forgiveness for the complacency we sometimes fall into concerning blatant sin. Please purify our own hearts and guide us in interceding for our nation. May America one day resound with the joy of returning to You, Lord!

And they told me, "The remnant who survived the exile are there in the province, in great trouble and disgrace. The wall of Jerusalem is broken down, and its gates are burned with fire." When I heard these words, I sat down and wept. I mourned for days, fasting and praying before the God of heaven.

At the dedication of the wall of Jerusalem, the Levites were sought out from all their homes and brought to Jerusalem to celebrate the joyous dedication with thanksgiving and singing, accompanied by cymbals, harps, and lyres.

Nehemiah 1:3-4, 12:27

WHO WEEPS?

Who weeps? Who prays? Who intercedes?
Who, on his knees, to the Lord God pleads?
Who weeps? Who prays? Who cares today
that America has gone astray,
that sin runs rampant through our land?
Who will rise and take a stand?

Lord, You speak to us today.
"Rise and take a stand," You say.
Teach us, Lord, to weep and pray,

confess that we have gone astray.
Can two women intercede?
We stand to follow. We know You'll lead.

You lead Nehemiah to rebuild a wall,
to surround Jerusalem to prevent its fall.
You lead us to teach Your word today
and disciple others to seek You and pray.
As we exhort others for You to stand,
we trust in You to heal our land.

May American Christians humbly pray,
repent of sin and seek Your face.
As You restore us, may our joy overflow
that far and wide men will hear it and know
that the rejoicing of Your people, Lord,
is the answer to the promise in Your Word.

REJOICE! NATION SAVED FROM ANNIHILATION!

Mordecai went out from the presence of the king in royal garments of blue and white, with a large gold crown and a purple robe of fine linen. And the city of Susa shouted and rejoiced[H6670]. For the Jews it was a time of light and gladness[H8057], of joy[H8342] and honor. In every province and every city, wherever the king's edict and decree reached, there was joy[H8057] and gladness[H8342] among the Jews, with feasting and celebrating. And many of the people of the land themselves became Jews, because the fear of the Jews had fallen upon them.

Esther 8:15-17

Esther is the only book of the Bible in which God's name is never mentioned. However, we see the divine orchestration of events as He uses a beautiful young Jewish woman and her "bonus father" to save His people. Esther's parents died, and she was raised by her relative Mordecai in the capital city of Susa in Persia. You may recall that she won the position of Queen to King Ahasuerus (Xerxes) by a landslide in a huge beauty pageant! After she became Queen, Mordecai learned that an evil man named Haman had convinced the king—who did not know his Queen was Jewish—to order that all Jews be slaughtered on a specific day. After three days of fasting—prayer is not specified but was usually the reason for a fast—courageous Queen Esther approached the throne without being summoned which could result in the death penalty. She asked the king and Haman to attend a feast, then a second feast. At the second feast she begged the king for the lives of her people, revealing that she was Jewish and exposing Haman for the villain he was. The king stormed out, and Haman groveled at the feet of Esther. The king returned, saw the scene, and ordered Haman executed for attempting to violate Queen Esther. Haman was hanged on the 50-ft-gallows he had built to hang Mordecai! Mordecai was elevated in the king's court, but he and Esther still needed to save their lives as well as those of all the Jews captive in provinces belonging to King Ahasuerus. King Ahasuerus reminded Esther and Mordecai how he had recompensed them by turning over Haman's property to them and that once something like Haman's order that the Jews be killed is sealed with the king's signet ring, it cannot be nullified. He gave his blessing for them to write a new order that would rectify the situation and seal it with his ring. He gave them carte blanche to compose a plan that would save his queen and her people. Mordecai was the author of these new orders, and the king dispatched them by the fastest means available, couriers riding the best horses sired by his own stud horse. He wanted to get the message out quickly for the Jews to have adequate time to prepare. The new edict, worded much the same as the original, gave the Jews the right to fight back and even confiscate the spoils, making it a fair fight instead of a virtual slaughter of the Jews. Mordecai was elevated from sackcloth and ashes to royal robes, and the Jews celebrate the Feast of Purim to this day to remember how Esther saved the nation from annihilation. Mordecai demonstrated faith when he prophesied that Esther was promoted to queen for this critical time.

Esther 4:14 *For if you remain silent at this time, relief and deliverance for the Jews will arise from another place, but you and your father's house will perish. And who knows if perhaps you have come to the kingdom for such a time as this?*

Look for how God has used seemingly unrelated circumstances to bring you to your current situation in life. Trust Him to direct your path, and do not take another step without seeking His will and way.

Father, give us faith to see that our circumstances are not coincidental and may be Your way of directing us to glorify Your name and lead others to trust in You!

GOD'S PRUNING PRODUCES JOY

But let all who take refuge in You rejoice[H8055]; let them ever shout for joy[H7422]. May You shelter them, that those who love Your name may rejoice[H5970] in You. For surely You, O LORD, bless the righteous; You surround them with the shield of Your favor.

Psalm 5:11-12

> Refuge – That which shelters or protects from danger, distress or calamity; a stronghold which protects by its strength, or a sanctuary which secures safety by its sacredness; any place inaccessible to an enemy. (17)

The Lord is the definition of refuge; His very essence is protection and a sacred place to abide. Therefore, we can celebrate the Lord with joyful singing and praises. God offers us a place of safety so that we who adore Him may glorify Him. God brings joy to His family of faith. The Lord promotes us, elevates us, and is our defense. Our joy reverberates back toward Him and has a ripple effect that touches others. The year that I (Susan) was turning thirteen, I was sent to a therapeutic boarding school almost 400 miles away from home. I knew no one there except the Lord Jesus. He was my only and definite Protector. At the time, I felt frustrated, angry, and abandoned. However, after I set these emotions aside, I realized that it was God's compassion, concern, and grace that had brought me to that place and was thankful the Lord's providence sent me there. The sudden separation from my family ultimately produced pruning for both personal and spiritual growth. My roots grew deep in my Lord, which caused me to blossom. Refinement causes discomfort even to the point of pain, but the final result is fruitfulness. God helped me to discover my love for learning to a greater measure and used caring teachers like Gail Meaux to help me uncover my gift for communication through words. He gave me my first "bonus sister" in soul and spirit in Missy Blanchard. He gave me nurses like Ethel Rawls and Patti Hearne who nurtured my emotional and spiritual wellbeing along with taking care of my physical needs. He brought me a fantastic encourager in the form of Patti's husband, George. The school I first viewed as a punishment was used by God to be my refuge and shelter. "I am the true vine, and my Father is the vinedresser. Every branch in Me that does not bear fruit, He takes away; and every branch that bears fruit, He prunes it so that it may bear more fruit" (John 15:1-2 ESV). God pruned away the resentment of feeling like I was ejected from my home to make me more productive and fruitful in my witness for Him.

Do you trust the Master Gardener or are you shrinking away from His pruning shears? Do you see God as your sanctuary when life is difficult? Trust in Him and rejoice!

Father, thank You that we can trust You to use even the difficult times in our lives to mold us into the image of Your Son (Romans 8:28-29).

JOY IN HIS PRESENCE, NOW AND FOREVER

I have set the LORD always before me. Because He is at my right hand, I will not be shaken. Therefore my heart is glad[H8055] and my tongue rejoices[H1523]; my body also will dwell securely. For You will not abandon my soul to Sheol, nor will You let Your Holy One see decay. You have made known to me the path of life; You will fill me with joy[H8057] in Your presence, with eternal pleasures at Your right hand.

Psalm 16:8-11

> 16:10 These words expressed the confidence of the lesser David, but were applied messianically to the resurrection of the Greater David (the Lord Jesus Christ) both by Peter (Acts 2:25–28) and Paul (Acts 13:35). (18)

After Peter quoted Psalm 16 in Acts 2:25-28, he went on to explain that David was speaking prophetically about the Messiah, Jesus, when he wrote it:

Acts 2:29-32 Brothers, I can tell you with confidence that the patriarch David died and was buried, and his tomb is with us to this day. But he was a prophet and knew that God had promised him on oath that He would place one of his descendants on his throne. Foreseeing this, David spoke about the resurrection of the Christ, that He was not abandoned to Hades, nor did

His body see decay. God has raised this Jesus to life, to which we are all witnesses.

David found his security and joy in the Lord and shares that testimony in Psalm 16. Verse 10 is Messianic prophecy concerning the resurrection of Jesus but is also true of believers. Even though our physical "earth-suits" will die and decay, who we are immediately enters the presence of the Lord; and when He returns, our bodies will be raised and transformed into glorious, incorruptible bodies!

Acts 15:51-52 *Listen, I tell you a mystery: We will not all sleep, but we will all be changed—in an instant, in the twinkling of an eye, at the last trumpet. For the trumpet will sound, the dead will be raised imperishable, and we will be changed.*

Even now, we are dwelling together with the Lord through the presence of the Holy Spirit in our lives. He is instructing and guiding us in the way that we should live. As we walk in obedience to His instruction manual for our lives—the Bible— He brings us totality of peace, love, and joy. "If you keep My commandments, you will remain in My love, just as I have kept My Father's commandments and remain in His love." (John 15:10). From God's seat of authority, He bestows eternal joy to His treasured ones who are saved by His grace. I have joy right now because God, in His great magnificence, uses me when I am yielded, listening, and obedient. I trust and know that this life is only a "way station" on my journey to my everlasting home. I look forward to streets of gold and gates of pearl, to the sheer beauty of being in His presence. I will enjoy being able to move freely, dancing before the Lord while playing an instrument to praise Him. In my glorified body, I will need no glasses. Perhaps I will not have an overbite and will have wisdom without the gray hair!

Have you surrendered to the Lord's call to follow Him? In addition to the security of knowing Heaven will be your forever home, do you also enjoy basking in the Lord's presence here and now in your day-to-day life? Like David, have you "set the Lord always before you"? Are you practicing the command of Hebrews 12:2: "Let us fix our eyes on Jesus, the author and perfecter of our faith, who for the joy set before Him endured the cross, scorning its shame, and sat down at the right hand of the throne of God."? Christ's death and resurrection meant that Jesus would no longer be an only child. It also meant that those of us who trust in Him will never be orphans, because our Father God keeps us securely in His forever family.

Father, thank You for the security of being in Your presence both now and forever.

Worship with The Martins singing "In the Presence of Jehovah:" https://www.youtube.com/watch?v=EqiLW-WxZulM

*Protect me, God, for you are my refuge. I said to Adonai,
"You are my Lord; I have nothing good outside of you."
The holy people in the land are the ones who are worthy of honor; all my pleasure[H2656] is in them. . . I always
set Adonai before me; with him at my right hand, I can
never be moved; so my heart is glad[H8055], my glory rejoices[H1523], and my body too rests in safety; for you will
not abandon me to Sh'ol, you will not let your faithful
one see the Abyss. You make me know the path of life;
in your presence is unbounded joy[H8057], in your right
hand eternal delight[H5273].*

Psalm 16:1-3, 8-11 (CJB)

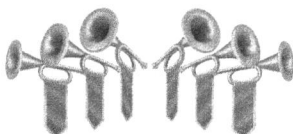

JOY IN YOUR PRESENCE, NOW AND ALWAYS

Lord, You are my protector, my strong defender,
the Giver of everything perfect and good.
I enjoy "familyship" with Your people, Oh God,
those trusting in You, living as they should.
I focus on You, Lord, Your will and Your ways.
Standing firm by Your side, I will not be defeated.
I rejoice in Your presence. You are with me always.
I am safe and secure 'til my days are completed.
When my life is over and this earth-suit is buried,
my soul and spirit won't taste death or decay;
for through saving faith in Jesus, I have life eternal,
perpetual joy in Your presence now and always.

FAITH IS THE VICTORY

May He give you the desires of your heart and make all your plans succeed. May we shout for joy^{H7442} at your victory and raise a banner in the name of our God. May the LORD grant all your petitions.

Psalm 20:4-5

20:1 you. The king. The congregation calls upon the Lord to bless the king as he sets out for war. The blessings in these verses are also properly applied to New Testament believers in their battle of faith. (19)

1 John 5:3-5 *For this is the love of God, that we keep His commandments. And His commandments are not burdensome, because everyone born of God overcomes the world. And this is the victory that has overcome the world: our faith. Who then overcomes the world? Only he who believes that Jesus is the Son of God.*

The people of Israel prayed for their king to be protected and victorious in battle. They promised to rejoice over the victory they were confident their God would provide. Those of us who have trusted Jesus for salvation—victory—are confident that He will prevail in this world. Today's circumstances may appear to be bleak and discouraging—Covid-19 pandemic, Russia waging war against Ukraine, moral decline of America, war in Israel. However, our joy is not dependent upon circumstances—current, past, or future. Our joy is determined by dependence upon the Lord Jesus Christ's fulfillment of His Father's assignment: 1) He died the most horrendous and humiliating death known at that time to pay the price for our sin, 2) He rose from the tomb to conquer death and the grave to be the firstfruits of the resurrection, 3) He is now seated at the right hand of the Father, the place of authority, and intercedes for His inheritance—those who have trusted in Him—constantly, 4) He sent the Holy Spirit to live in us as a down payment assuring us of our final victory to be with Him in paradise forever. We rejoice in His victory and have joy knowing we will be victorious because of Jesus. In fact, as far as God is concerned, we are already there!

Ephesians 2:4-6 *But because of His great love for us, God, who is rich in mercy, made us alive with Christ even when we were dead in our trespasses. It is by grace you have been saved! And God raised us up with Christ and seated us with Him in the heavenly realms in Christ Jesus . . .*

Are the current world or even personal circumstances attempting to rob you of your joy? Is the enemy trying to defeat you through health or financial problems, or despair over the state of your nation? Remind yourself that true joy is found in the Lord and His promises. Read and memorize Scripture verses that remind you who you are in Christ (Ephesians is a good place to start). Begin each day affirming that you will rejoice in the victory of the

King of kings, and Lord of lords; for your King is the highest and greatest of all!

Father, You make us victorious over the world and all its influence when we remain centered in Your will. Help us to know the joy of Your victory as we go through each day!

Worship with choir from Fountainview Academy singing "Faith is the Victory": https://www.youtube.com/watch?v=DSNMQAVe7FE

JOY IN GOD'S STRENGTH SALVATION, AND PRESENCE

O LORD, the king rejoices[H8055] *in Your strength. How greatly he exults*[H1523] *in Your salvation! You have granted his heart's desire and have not withheld the request of his lips. Selah*

For You welcomed him with rich blessings; You placed on his head a crown of pure gold. He asked You for life, and You granted it—length of days, forever and ever. Great is his glory in Your salvation; You bestow on him splendor and majesty.

For You grant him blessings forever; You cheer him with joy[H8057] *in Your presence. For the king trusts in the LORD; through the loving devotion of the Most High, he will not be shaken.*

Psalm 21:5-7

21:2 his heart's desire. Similar language is used in 20:4, though it is uncertain whether the same occasion inspired both psalms. The first part of Ps. 21 sounds like the answer to the prayer in Ps. 20. (20)

21:4 In response to the king's request for preservation God gave him life—yes, length of days forever and ever. This latter expression probably means long life in David's case, but it is literally true of the endless resurrection life of the Messiah. (21)

King David rejoiced in the Lord's strength, salvation, and presence. He praised the Lord for making him victorious in battle, for blessing him, and for the gift of long life. David did live a long life on earth and is now with his Lord for eternity. However, the "length of days, forever and ever" probably refers to the length of the Davidic dynasty in which the Messiah, Jesus, will reign eternally. Exactly what did David do to earn these blessings from God? He trusted God. Period. End of story. Yes, David gave sacrifices, and participated in the annual feasts, but these are not what gained God's favor. David placed his trust, his life, the totality of his being in the hands of his loving Lord. David was completely dependent on His lovingly devoted God to sustain him. Similarly, we do not earn salvation through good works. We place our trust in Jesus Christ alone who died to purchase our redemption from slavery to sin. Jesus satisfied the wrath of God on our behalf, and all we have to "do" is answer His call by placing our complete trust in Him. Then He will bless us to win the daily battles against the influence of this world and our enemy, Satan, in order to do what He calls us to do. He has blessed us with length of days forever because we will be resurrected and given an incorruptible (indestructible) body when He returns.

We can rejoice in the Lord's strength to sustain us, salvation to deliver us, and presence to guide us just as David did because He is still lovingly devoted to His children. Have you had a praise party yet today? Take a moment to meditate on the joy that is ours because of Christ. As brother Jimmy Draper used to say, "If that don't light your fire, your wood's wet!"

Father, we rejoice in the reality that we can place our total dependence on You and know that we will not be shaken from our faith because You will enable us to stand (Romans 14:4). Our wood is dry and burning brightly to light the way to You for others.

GOD IS MY ROCK AND MY SHELTER

For in the day of trouble He will hide me in His shelter; He will conceal me under the cover of His tent; He will set me high upon a rock. Then my head will be held high above my enemies around me. At His tabernacle I will offer sacrifices with shouts of joy[H8643]; I will sing and make music to the LORD.

Psalm 27:5-6

Psalm 27:6 Confident of God's care and help in trouble, the psalmist anticipates victory over those who have troubled God's people. He vows to sacrifice to the Lord to express his devotion, while singing a hymn to his God. Doubtless he proclaims the mighty acts of God's redemption in his "shouts of joy" and song, in anticipation of victory. His expressions of loyalty result from a trusting heart. (22)

King David was a living hymnal. He composed many of the Psalms which were sung in worship at the tabernacle, later in the Temple, and in the time of Christ, at synagogues. David is confident that his Lord will shield him from his enemies and place him "high on a rock." High ground is more easily defended, but God Himself was David's rock. There is no safer place to be than in the Lord's hands (John 10:27-30). David's total trust was in God. Therefore, he could be confident that he would bring sacrifices to the Lord, singing and shouting for joy victoriously. Because David sought the Lord's face—His presence—within the tabernacle and enjoyed an intense relationship with his God; what he saw outside the canvas of the tabernacle did not shake or move him. Enemies and adverse circumstances could surround him, but his confidence in the Lord's protection did not waver. Jesus is our rock, our safe place, and our firm foundation. Our "house" will not fall because our trust is in Him (Matthew 7:24-25). We can go through our days with joy and confidence in the Lord's ability to preserve us until the time He has chosen to take us to the home He is preparing for us (John 14:1-3).

Is your heart troubled? Do the day-to-day worries of this earthly life keep you awake at night? Has the Enemy—Satan—succeeded in temporarily robbing you of your joy? We hope these devotions focusing on joy will invigorate you and restore your confidence in the Source of joy—Jesus Christ! Like the wise man in the parable, build your house on the Rock of your salvation, then trust in Him to keep it standing.

Father, Jesus is our Rock and the firm foundation upon which we build our lives. Help us to remember to run to You in difficult times and continue to sing joyfully even if everything seems to be falling apart around us. Our circumstances do not create joy: You do!

Joyfully sing along in worship with Whitney Houston singing "I Go to the Rock" by Dottie Rambo:

https://www.youtube.com/watch?v=TpP1oaNWtKA

JOYFUL SONG OF THANKSGIVING

The LORD is my strength and my shield; my heart trusts in Him, and I am helped. Therefore my heart rejoices,[H5937] and I give thanks to Him with my song.

Psalm 28:7

David had many times when he needed God to be his strength and shield. Enemies pursued him (it seemed regularly) and even his own son Absolom raised an army against him. David always remembered his strength came from God. Even as a boy he slayed the Giant Goliath with God's strength behind the stone as it hurled out of his sling. His confidence was bolstered by the fact that God had already delivered him from wild beasts while tending his father's sheep.

1 Samuel 17:45 *But David said to the Philistine, "You come against me with sword and spear and javelin, but I come against you in the name of the LORD of Hosts, the God of the armies of Israel, whom you have defied.*

David was God's warrior, but he was also God's singer who glorified the Lord with psalms. God has never had to rescue me (Susie) from wild animals or help me to fight a nine-foot-tall giant, but God has been my strength and shield. When my husband left me, I battled a deep depression and even questioned how my loving God could let divorce happen to me. I cried out to the

Lord . . . actually I yelled at Him. He heard my cries and guided me to a Christian singles group who loved me, discipled me, and restored my trust in the God of my salvation. God had to restore not only my trust in Him but my ability to trust and let other people in. The person I had pledged my love to, with whom I had become one flesh, had deserted me. Gradually, that trust in God and His people grew in me again. As I healed from my hurts, my songs of joy were restored. I once again rejoiced to express gratitude to the Lord with my voice and my piano. Psalm 28:7 became my favorite verse and a memorized reminder in the tough times, that the Lord IS my strength and my shield, and I can trust Him.

Are you going through a time when it is difficult to find a reason to give thanks joyfully? Make a practice of giving thanks for even the tiniest blessings—a beautiful flower in your garden, a child waving at you in the grocery store, the ability to pay your bills on time. I have found that as I express gratitude to God, He gives me more reasons to be grateful. Think back on previous times you thought you couldn't go on, but God intervened through the thoughtfulness of a friend or the kindness of a stranger. Make thanksgiving a habit, and the Lord will restore your joy.

Lord, help us to count and be thankful for our blessings rather than wallow in our woes. You are "a shield around me, my glory, and the One who lifts my head" (Psalm 3:3). Increase our faith in You that we may re-

sist being discouraged and drink up the encouragement found in Your sweet word.

JOY RESTORED

Sing to the LORD, O you His saints, and praise His holy name. For His anger is fleeting, but His favor lasts a lifetime. Weeping may stay the night, but joy[H7440] comes in the morning.

Psalm 30:4-5

H7440 *rinnâh* ¬– from H7442; properly, a creaking: -(or shrill sound), i.e. shout (of joy or grief):— cry, gladness, joy, proclamation, rejoicing, shouting, sing(-ing), triumph. (23)

David thanked God for freedom from his murderous enemies. He says for the righteous to rejoice in song and offer gratitude in the awesome name of the Lord. God's chastisement is temporal, but His blessing is without end. Wailing is fed by darkness, but joy feeds on the Light. In John 8:12, Jesus said, "I am the light of the world. Whoever follows Me will never walk in the darkness, but will have the light of life." Our focus as believers is to be on Jesus alone. He is the Light who enables us to shout for joy.

In November of 1992, I (Susan) went through a horrific, heartbreaking experience with a young man who had discussed engagement with me. We thought we were in love. We had been best friends for four-and-a-half years before we began dating. I come from divorced parents, so we met with our pastors to ask them to pray and to give us their feelings on the matter even before we started dating. We received their blessing. I felt the Lord had impressed upon me in August that I needed to break up with him or my heart would be shattered, but I did not obey. I was having too much fun thinking that I was in love to listen to the One who loved me more than anyone else. At the time, the truth that God had revealed to me in August was so deeply buried in my heart that I did not admit it to myself. Months earlier, my boyfriend's family had bought tickets so that he could spend our three-week Christmas vacation with me and my family. Then on Thanksgiving weekend (also finals week of my first semester of graduate school), out of the blue, with no apparent warning, my best friend/boyfriend broke up with me and told me he wanted to see other people. This shattered me. However, the Lord had warned me, but I chose to be in denial. To make a much longer story short, the reason I survived this awfully terrible breakup is that Jesus tenderly came to me through an adopted family, whom He used to put my broken heart back together again. Joy came because I had that "framily" who lovingly, prayerfully, and tenderly came alongside me until I could once again lift my head to see the light of the morning.

Are you struggling with a painful breakup or other difficult problem? Let Jesus shine His light on the situation and strengthen you with the true Light. He will restore your joy!

Father, in our darkest moments, help us to remember that Jesus is the Light!

Worship and rejoice with Baylor Wilson singing "Joy Comes in the Morning": https://www.youtube.com/watch?v=_sGtUWzaJ3E

RIGHT RELATIONSHIP WITH GOD RESULTS IN JOY

Be glad[H8055] in the LORD and rejoice[H1523], O righteous ones; shout for joy[H7442], all you upright in heart.

Psalm 32:11

David is laying everything out on the table, prostrating himself before the divine court for mercy. He had an adulterous relationship with Bathsheba and orchestrated the murder of her husband, Uriah the Hittite, who was one of David's mighty men. When David's sin and God's holiness were contradictory to one another, he experienced ailments, and his strength was draining away in immeasurable proportions. But when he admitted the sins God was addressing, he was met not with retribution but with redemption. In this psalm, David celebrates the undeserved forgiveness that his gracious Father extended with no strings attached.

Lack of obedience is disobedience which is sin. God had called me, Susan Slade, to be his teaching preacher and His megaphone. I knew in 1982 that this was what I was supposed to do, but I was resistant and, therefore, disobedient because of tradition. At that point, I was willing to let the tradition of male ministers only take precedence over God's authority in my life. I also reminded the Lord that I was disabled as if He didn't know how he made me. I was limiting my thinking to the job of pastor. I had no vision in 1982 of teaching and preaching through writing and use of the internet. Something transpired in my life in 1988 that caused me to say, "Okay, God, whatever You want." I am not implying that God caused what happened. I am saying that because of what happened, I wanted to be sure that God and I were on the same page. When I said, "Yes," to God completely, I knew that whatever happened, because I was obedient to God, He would have my back.

Are you resisting God's prodding in a particular situation? You will experience freedom once you surrender to His authority. He will then enable you to do all He has called you to do.

Father, help us to recognize when You are calling us to a specific purpose and give us the courage to surrender to Your will immediately. Thank You for forgiving us when we are too stubborn to submit to Your calling immediately the moment You impress it upon our hearts.

JOYFULLY USE YOUR GIFTS TO GLORIFY GOD

Rejoice[H7442] in the LORD, O righteous ones; it is fitting for the upright to praise Him. Praise the LORD with the harp; make music to Him with ten strings. Sing to Him a new song; play skillfully with a shout of joy[H8643].

Psalm 33:1-3

H8643 *tᵉrûw'âh* - from H7321; clamor, i.e. acclamation of joy or a battle-cry; especially clangor of trumpets, as an alarm:—alarm, blow(-ing) (of, the) (trumpets), joy, jubilee, loud noise, rejoicing, shout(-ing), (high, joyful) sound(-ing). (24)

We exalt the name of the Lord because we are His creation, and He sustains us (Hebrews 1:1-3). All instruments—voices and those made of wood, strings, and metals—can be used to glorify God. Never be satisfied with half-hearted, mediocre effort and devotion when using the talents and gifts that are blessings from God. However, do not let your performance skills outweigh your jubilation in the Spirit. We have many reasons to rejoice. We have the truth of God's word. God is trustworthy. The Lord is impartial and equitable in all things, and He desires those qualities in His children. God's love for us is relentless and tenacious. His love never fails.

I (Susan) am not gifted with melody or song, but I do seek to exalt and glorify the Lord with poetry that encourages and exhorts others. One example is something I call "champion blessings." The Lord impressed upon me that there were many children I knew who were facing various challenges—physical, mental, or emotional. I pray for them and seek the Lord for inspiration to write an acrostic poem based on their names. I have now expanded this line of poetry to include all children because they all face challenges each day. These poems are rooted in verses of Scripture to focus the children and/or their families on God's design for His children rather than the adversities they face.

Has the Lord gifted you with an ability that is lying dormant? Allow Him to mold it into something for His purposes and the benefit of others. Then exercise that gift joyfully to glorify God!

Father, we thank You for giving us a gift for using words to encourage and instruct others. Help us always to use these gifts to glorify Your name. We thank You for the joy that exercising our God-given gifts brings to us.

Worship along with Phil Driscoll singing "I Exalt Thee": https://www.youtube.com/watch?v=Hs1umL5x7rQ

RADIANT WITH JOY: SPARKLING!!!

I will bless the LORD at all times; His praise will always be on my lips. My soul boasts in the LORD; let the oppressed hear and rejoice[H8055]. Magnify the LORD with me; let us exalt His name together. I sought the LORD, and He answered me; He delivered me from all my fears. Those who look to Him are radiant with joy[H5102]; their faces shall never be ashamed.

Psalm 34:1-5

> H5102 *nâhar*, naw-har'; a primitive root; to sparkle, i.e. (figuratively) be cheerful; hence (from the sheen of a running stream) to flow, i.e. (figuratively) assemble:—flow (together), be lightened. (25)

Hebrews 1:3a The Son is the radiance of God's glory and the exact representation of His nature.

Romans 8:29 For those God foreknew, He also predestined to be conformed to the image of His Son, so that He would be the firstborn among many brothers.

Malachi 3:17a (AMPC) And they shall be Mine, says the Lord of hosts, in that day when I publicly recognize and openly declare them to be My jewels (My special possession, My peculiar treasure).

"Those who look to Him are radiant with joy"—sparkling! In Malachi 3:17, those who were loyal to the Lord, who did not chase after idols but remained faithful to the one true God, He called his "jewels." Multi-faceted jewels sparkle; they shine; they reflect the light around them. Jesus is described as "the radiance of God's glory and the exact representation of His nature." Jesus radiates the glory, love, and grace of the Father. Those of us who have been chosen by God, who have trusted Jesus as Savior and Lord—both men and women—are in the process of being "conformed to the image" of God's Son, Jesus. If Jesus is the radiance of God's glory, we are the Lord's precious jewels, reflecting that glory and sparkling in a dark world. We stand out in this fallen world because we give off the light of Jesus's love. In John 8:12, Jesus described Himself as the "Light of the world," and in Matthew 5:14, Jesus told His disciples, "You are the light of the world." We are to reflect the light of God's glory, grace, and love to a lost and dying world. Our purpose is to joyfully sparkle!

Do you see yourself as a precious, priceless, sparkling jewel in the treasury of God? Do you realize that is the transformation that is taking place in your life? Perhaps you feel like you once sparkled but need to be cleaned up and polished. If so, apply 1 John 1:9, "If we confess our sins, He is faithful and just to forgive us our sins and to cleanse us from all unrighteousness." God is willing and able to buff, polish, and sometimes grind off a layer to restore your sparkle that you may shine as His light in your part of this world. Sparkling does not depend on our surroundings or circumstances. Light seems brighter in an extremely dark place. When all around you seems dull and dim, trust in Jesus and keep on sparkling!

Father, we know we are Your precious jewels. May that radiance be seen on our faces, and sparkle in our interactions with others. May people be drawn to You because they see the reflection of Jesus in us.

Worship with Joni Eareckson Tada and the Gaither Homecoming singing "When He Cometh": https://www.youtube.com/watch?v=8fXDd72bKUk
Lyrics are printed for you on the next page:

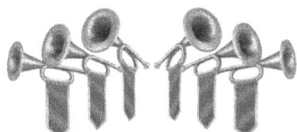

When He Cometh

By William Cushing (1823-1902)

When He cometh, when He cometh
To make up His jewels,
All His jewels, precious jewels,
His loved and His own:

Like the stars of the morning,
His bright crown adorning,
They shall shine in their beauty,
Bright gems for His crown.

He will gather, He will gather
The gems for His kingdom;
All the pure ones, all the bright ones,
His loved and His own.

Like the stars of the morning,
His bright crown adorning,
They shall shine in their beauty,
Bright gems for His crown.

Little children, little children,
Who love their Redeemer,
Are the jewels, precious jewels,
His loved and His own.

Like the stars of the morning,
His bright crown adorning,
They shall shine in their beauty,
Bright gems for His crown.

Those who look to Him are radiant with joy[H5102]; their faces shall never be ashamed.

Psalm 34:5

SPARKLE

Shine as God's radiant jewel. *Malachi 3:17a*

Pray for the Lord to polish you. *1 John 1:9*

Apart from Christ you can do nothing. *John 15:5b*

Reflect the image of Jesus. *Romans 8:29a*

King Jesus rejoices over you. *Zephaniah 3:17b*

Lord, we rejoice in Your presence. *Psalm 16:11b*

Eternal One, pinnacle of our joy. *Psalm 43:4a*

"BAD TO THE BONE" VS JOY TO THE BONES!

May their path be dark and slick, as the angel of the LORD pursues. For without cause they laid their net for me; without reason they dug a pit for my soul. May ruin befall them by surprise; may the net they hid ensnare them; may they fall into the hazard they created. Then my soul will rejoice[H1523] in the LORD and exult[H7797] in His salvation. All my bones will exclaim, "Who is like You, O LORD, who delivers the afflicted from the aggressor, the poor and needy from the robber?" . . .

May those who favor my vindication shout for joy[H7442] and gladness[H8055]; may they always say, "Exalted be the LORD who delights in His servant's well-being." Then my tongue will proclaim Your righteousness and Your praises all day long.

Psalm 35:7-10, 27-28

Proverbs 17:22 *A joyful heart is good medicine, but a broken spirit dries up the bones.*

We are not sure when "Bad to the bone" became a slang expression for something really good. We find it annoying the way vocabulary is flipped to no longer mean what it once did. The Psalmist prayed for deliverance and proclaimed that even his bones would praise the Lord! Arthritis makes our bones hurt, and depression is sometimes felt to the bone. However, joy can be felt to that depth as well. Our Lord delivers us not only from our slavery to sin, but many times from poverty, depression, and sometimes even literal enemies. Pain and affliction can plague deeply, but joy can penetrate to the cellular level as well! The overcomer can shout joyfully in victory despite persistent pain. When we feel powerless over our pain, Jesus is still omnipotent—all-powerful. As Paul wrote, "But He said to me, 'My grace is sufficient for you, for My power is perfected in weakness.' Therefore I will boast all the more gladly in my weaknesses, so that the power of Christ may rest on me" (2 Corinthians 12:9). I (Susan) may not always feel this Scripture in my earth-suit, but I trust and apply this verse to my life because feelings lie; but the word of God is always true.

Are you in pain? Are you facing a difficult situation? Has someone laid a trap to place blame on you falsely? Pray asking the Lord to deliver you. Then rejoice in anticipation of His answering your prayer. Take a moment to recount all the excellent things the Lord has done in your life and experience joy to the bones!

Father, we praise You right now because we can trust You to not only sustain us but bring us to a place of victory. Let us experience joy in Your grace and love that is felt even to our bones!

Worship for those who need encouragement "He'll do it Again" written by Shirley Ceasar, performed by unknown artist: https://www.youtube.com/watch?v=kt-V3Bm5DHZY

WRAP YOURSELF IN PRAYER

These things come to mind as I pour out my soul: how I walked with the multitude, leading the procession to the house of God with shouts of joy[H7440] and praise. Why are you downcast, O my soul? Why the unease within me? Put your hope in God, for I will yet praise Him for the salvation of His presence.

Psalm 42:4-5

HOPE – Confidence in a future event; the highest degree of well-founded expectation of good; as a hope founded on God's gracious promises; a scriptural sense. A well-founded scriptural hope is, in our religion, the source of ineffable happiness. (26)

INEFFABLE – adjective [Latin ineffabilis; in and effabilis, from effort, to speak.] Unspeakable; unutterable; that cannot be expressed in words; usually in a good sense; as the ineffable joys of heaven; the ineffable glories of the Deity. (27)

In Psalm 42, one of the sons of Korah reminds himself that he once had been the pied piper of the worshippers. However, at the time of writing this psalm, his soul was parched, anguished for the quenching power of the Lord's presence. His enemies constantly badgered and harassed him concerning God's seeming lack of faithfulness to him. They were in essence saying, "This best Friend of yours has abandoned you." The psalmist started to believe the taunting of the haters and asked the Lord, "Why have You forgotten me?" Then he asked himself, "Why are you behaving this way? Why are you drowning in a self-made pity party?" The psalmist turned his focus off of himself and off of his problems and onto his solution—the all-knowing, all-seeing, all-powerful God.

After graduation from ORU, I (Susan) moved from the vibrancy of campus life into an apartment building designed for the elderly and physically or mentally challenged. Many of my neighbors were severely mentally impaired, and if off their medications, could be frightening. I was in self-imposed isolation due to fear. I went through a deep depression, to the point that I hardly spoke except to talk to God in prayer because I was so depressed and felt empty. I don't even know how many months it lasted! I would pray, and I would cry. Then I would pray and cry some more. I would be frank with God in my heart because I reasoned that God knew anyway, so I might as well say what I was thinking and feeling. I couldn't hide anything from a God who knows everything. I was forthcoming about my pain, emotional as well as physical. The emotional even eclipsed the physical at that time. I can't even say when it began because I was praying continuously and crying out to God; but gradually, in the fullness of God's time, He was faithful to lift the cloud of depression. I was able to experience the effervescent exuberance of joy once again!

When you are in a time of despair, do not neglect to wrap yourself in prayer! At the appointed time, the Lord will lift your cares.

Father, we know we can cast all our cares on You (1 Peter 5:7), but sometimes we wallow in despair and defeat before we do so. Help us to exercise "self-talk" and prayer like this Psalmist to reaffirm and reinvigorate our trust and dependance on You.

GOD, MY GREATEST PLEASURE, AND THE PINNACLE OF MY JOY

Send out Your light and Your truth; let them lead me. Let them bring me to Your holy mountain, and to the place where You dwell. Then I will go to the altar of God, to God, my greatest joy^{H8057}. I will praise You with the harp, O God, my God.

Psalm 43:3–4

The psalmist asked God to send out His beacon to light the way into His presence. He asked the Lord to bring him "out of darkness into His marvelous light" (1 Peter 2:9). God was his overwhelming, glorious jubilation. God is not only the source of joy, but He is the essence, the totality, and the fabric of joy. The Lord inspired a spontaneous melody for the psalmist to play on the harp. The psalmist chose to demonstrate or share his reasons for joy even while still walking out of despair.

Practically my whole last undergraduate semester, I (Susan) had walking pneumonia, which doctors kept misdiagnosing. That was extremely frustrating. Finally, the doctor who normally saw me in the infirmary figured it out. He sent me home to bed and said that I was not supposed to get out for anything. My caveat to him was, "I am going to church because I need to be in an atmosphere of healing and praise." He reluctantly agreed. I went back to class slightly too soon, and my caring professor, Dr. Thorpe, sent me back home and told me in no uncertain terms not to come back to class or I was not going to graduate on time. This caused me to have to write my undergraduate senior project within a six-weeks' timeframe, rather than having the entire semester like everyone else had. That was terribly challenging. I thrived, despite the time limit, by the grace of God, and even got an A on content. God was my exceeding joy, for His extravagant grace enabled me to graduate on time.

Are you rejoicing in a goal accomplished? Give God the glory for seeing you through and praise the Lord that He is the pinnacle of your joy!

Father, thank You that even in the worst circumstances, You give us joy. You are our exceeding joy!

OIL OF JOY

You have loved righteousness and hated wickedness; therefore God, your God, has anointed you above your companions with the oil of joy^H8342. All your garments are fragrant with myrrh and aloes and cassia; from palaces of ivory the harps make you glad^H8055. All glorious is the princess in her chamber; her gown is embroidered with gold. In colorful garments she is led to the king; her virgin companions are brought before you. They are led in with joy^H8057 and gladness^H1524; they enter the palace of the king.

Psalm 45:7-8, 13-15

This is a wedding song for a king, but it is also a messianic prophecy. Kings were anointed at their inauguration and grooms at their weddings. The bride would leave her parents' home to move into a place the groom had prepared for her at his father's house. The bride of Christ leaves all to follow Him, and Jesus is now preparing a place for us in His Father's house. When Jesus ascended to Heaven, God showered Him with the oil of joy. Other kings were anointed with joy, but Jesus had a rushing waterfall of glad tidings and exuberant celebration recognizing Him as the King of all kings. Because Jesus walked on earth in a spirit of humility and complete obedience to His Father, God elevated the Son to the highest position of authority.

Philippians 2:8-11 *And being found in appearance as a man, He humbled Himself and became obedient to death—even death on a cross. Therefore God exalted Him to the highest place and gave Him the name above all names, that at the name of Jesus every knee should bow, in heaven and on earth and under the earth, and every tongue confess that Jesus Christ is Lord, to the glory of God the Father.*

Our Groom, Jesus, eagerly awaits the joyful reunion with His bride, the church, when we will share in His overwhelming delight forever. Are you longing to be with your First Love in His Father's house eternally? Have you studied, as a believer, about where you will be for eternity? If not, look in God's instruction manual, the Bible, to see what He says about the place He is creating for you. Look up "heaven" in a good concordance. Here are a couple of passages to get you started: John 14:1-6 and Revelation 21:19-25. We also recommend the book *Heaven* by Randy Alcorn.

Father, we eagerly anticipate the day we will stand before Jesus and be welcomed into our forever home. Meanwhile, help us to follow His example of humility and obedience while we are faithfully serving You in this world. Anoint us with the oil of Your joy as a witness to those who do not yet know Jesus.

Worship with Hubert C. singing "Oil of Joy"
https://www.youtube.com/watch?v=nVd3_1wvtCw

RIPPLES OF REJOICING

Clap your hands, all you peoples; shout[H7321] unto God with a voice of triumph[H7440]. God has ascended amid shouts of joy[H8643], the LORD with the sound of the horn. Sing praises to God, sing praises; sing praises to our King, sing praises! For God is King of all the earth; sing profound praises to Him.

Psalm 47:1, 5-7

Our cry of gladness and victory should reverberate or ripple throughout everything. Our entire being has the capacity to erupt in exuberant praise. This is a portrait of the intimate interaction between Jesus and His bride. We actively participate in demonstrating our love with our heart, mind, body, and soul. This is a shout from the rooftops like a blast of a trumpet with waves of sound carrying for miles. We are going to the mountaintops and declaring our affection for the Lord because of His triumph over sin and death. The next few verses of this psalm explore God's sovereignty, His power, and His authority to shape our destinies. He purposed in His heart to shape the destinies of His children as far back as creation. He decided our purposes and our ability to emit ripples of joy and praise before our conception:

Ephesians 1:3-6 *Blessed be the God and Father of our Lord Jesus Christ, who has blessed us in Christ with every spiritual blessing in the heavenly realms. For He chose us in Him before the foundation of the world to be holy and blameless in His presence. In love He predestined us for adoption as His sons through Jesus Christ, according to the good pleasure of His will, to the praise of His glorious grace, which He has freely given us in the Beloved One.*

Jeremiah 29:11 *For I know the plans I have for you, declares the LORD, plans to prosper you and not to harm you, to give you a future and a hope.*

We can rejoice through difficulties because even in the trying times, we see God's formation of the paths of purpose. If God gave His most excellent treasure—His only begotten Son Jesus—to live, love, and die for us, then how much more will He provide for us everything that we require to live joyously for Him? (Romans 8:31-32). Find your God-given passion and live it out as a vessel for the Lord's use. The Lord will create a wave of joy that expands outwardly from you as you serve Him faithfully. The ripples of our rejoicing should spread out to bless all who come into the sphere of our influence.

Father, may our joy be contagious! Help us to radiate the joy of the Lord like ripples on top of the water spreading exponentially.

As a father has compassion on his children, so the LORD has compassion on those who fear Him. For He knows our frame; He is mindful that we are dust.

Psalm 103:13-14

The LORD your God is among you; He is mighty to save. He will rejoice[H7797] over you with gladness[H8057]; He will quiet you with His love; He will rejoice[H1523] over you with singing.

Zephaniah 3:17

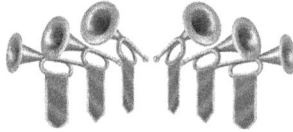

MY BONUS DAD
By Susan R. Slade

To help me understand our Father's love,
 the Lord blessed me with my bonus dad.
My bonus dad is compassionate and caring,
laughs when I'm joyful; comforts when I'm sad.
My bonus dad is only a letter or call away.
When I am in need of his godly advice,
the time he spends in counseling me
is a loving and willing sacrifice.
He rejoices with me in successes,
and embraces me with fatherly love.
My bonus dad is an earthly example
of our Heavenly Father above.

INTIMATELY ENGAGED WITH GOD ONCE AGAIN

Let me hear joy[H8342] and gladness[H8057]; let the bones You have crushed rejoice[H1523]. Restore to me the joy[H8342] of Your salvation, and sustain me with a willing spirit. Deliver me from bloodguilt, O God, the God of my salvation, and my tongue will sing[H7442] of Your righteousness.

Psalm 51:8, 12, 14

In Psalm 51, David puts all his cards on the table, lays his heart completely open, transparent to the Lord, within David's own humanity. Not only did David commit adultery with Bathsheba, but he conspired to have her husband, Uriah, murdered.

2 Samuel 11:14-15 *The next morning David wrote a letter to Joab and sent it with Uriah. In the letter he wrote: "Put Uriah at the front of the fiercest battle; then withdraw from him, so that he may be struck down and killed."*

Uriah had been one of David's mighty men, his completely loyal companions. In fact, David trusted Uriah to the point that he knew Uriah would not peak into a letter intended for Joab. Coldly, he had Uriah hand deliver the command that would have him murdered! Even though David knew that the all-knowing God saw his egregious sin, he openly and humbly confessed it in agreement with God's view of things. David had been devastated to the point of feeling crushed by the weight of his sin, but he had eager anticipation that God would bring him back into communion with Himself. David needed to be restored to be fit for holy service, and to be directed by the Holy Spirit. Then he would have the capacity to joyfully praise God because God and David would be intimately engaged once again.

Have you committed an overt sin in the past or failed to obey God completely, thus hindering the joy of your journey? Confess it, and by the power of His Spirit, turn back to the Lord. He will forgive you and cleanse you.

1 John 1:9 (AMPC) *If we [freely] admit that we have sinned and confess our sins, He is faithful and just (true to His own nature and promises) and will forgive our sins [dismiss our lawlessness] and [continuously] cleanse us from all unrighteousness [everything not in conformity to His will in purpose, thought, and action].*

God will restore your joy of being in right relationship with Him and bearing fruit for His glory. The Enemy, Satan, can no longer accuse you because you have been cleansed. You can stop Satan in his tracks by claiming the promise of 1 John 1:9.

Father, we know You see everything and know everything, but You instruct us to confess our sins to You. Therefore, we will be obedient to Your word and trust that when we confess, You will forgive us and make us brand new. You will restore us to the point of being fit for Your service and Your Kingdom. Thank You, Lord, that Your grace extends to us even though we were born sinners by nature.

David's confession in Psalm 51 set to music by John Michael Talbot: https://www.youtube.com/ watch?v=v8QlvvlaBnM

JOYOUS PROCLAMATION OF GOD'S DEVOTION

But I will sing of Your strength and proclaim^H7442 Your loving devotion in the morning. For You are my fortress, my refuge in times of trouble.

Psalm 59:16 (See 1 Samuel 19:1-24)

But as for me, I will sing about your power. Each morning I will sing with joy^H7442 about your unfailing love. For you have been my refuge, a place of safety when I am in distress.

Psalm 59:16 (NLT)

David's enemies were outside his door, ready to pounce like a pack of wild wolves. But David says (Susan paraphrase), "in the face of death, I will sing exuberantly in celebration of God's gracious, extravagant love." Similarly in Psalm 23, David writes that the Lord sets up a banquet table for him to dine leisurely in the middle of his enemies! God has been his place of safety while Saul plotted to have him murdered and sent his soldiers to execute his plan. Even though surrounded, David did not doubt God's power to deliver him.

My grandparents Bobby Joe and Helen Young—BJ and Nana— loved to travel. On one journey, they had an unplanned adventure. During the Cold War, they traveled to Germany and to Budapest, Hungary. BJ wanted to see the city of Leningrad (now St. Petersburg) because of its

historic significance during WWII, when the city was under siege for 872 days (nearly two and a half years). Because they had not been issued the proper visas to land in
Russia, they were surrounded by soldiers upon entering
the airport. The soldiers huddled up to decide what to do
with these two Americans. They seemed adamant that a
way must be found to get BJ and Nana out of Russia. At
first, my grandparents were told they would put them
on a ship to get them across the Baltic Sea and out of
Russia. Those in charge found a soldier who spoke good
English to guard my grandparents. Imagine—locked behind the Iron Curtain and uncertain of the outcome the
next day would hold. It was getting dark, and my grandparents had not had anything to eat. The soldier kindly
led them up some stairs to the kitchen, right past a room
with three red telephones, their command hotline, in
case of urgent official orders. My grandparents ate old,
stale, "hundred-year-old" cookies. To Nana's amazement, BJ witnessed to this English-speaking guard who
wanted to know all about the Savior he had only heard a
little about. Nana was praying as BJ shared, and Scripture seemed to roll off the tip of his tongue thanks to
the Holy Spirit. The guard wept as he realized the reality
that salvation could be his. His countenance was transformed as the Holy Spirit entered into his life. Nana was
excited and surprised at BJ witnessing so effectively. By
God's grace and providence, the guard was amazed that
BJ cared enough about him to share the truth about Jesus with him. The guard confided that he would never
be able to make enough money to buy a car or even the

gift he wished to give his bride-to-be. They all slept on hard benches that night until a flight the next day. Nana gave the guard, her newest brother in Christ, money to be able to buy a beautiful scarf as a wedding present for his fiancé.

No matter what enemies, evils, or fears surround us, God is faithful and just to deliver those who lean in on His grace. Do you have a fear, something that is over-whelming you? Lay it upon His broad shoulders. He is the only one who can carry the burden and pulverize its power over you. Then your life's joyful song of praise can resume.

Father, no matter what problems our enemy, Satan, surrounds us with, we will continue to joyfully, exuberantly sing Your praises by faith that You will conquer him and deliver us.

Worship with Janet Paschall, The Gaithers, and friends singing "He'll Deliver Me": https://www.youtube.com/watch?v=8mab7a-D88s

SHOUT FOR JOY!!!

*Those who live far away fear Your wonders; You make
the dawn and sunset shout for joy[H7442] . . .*

*The pastures of the wilderness overflow; the hills are
robed with joy[H1524]. The pastures are clothed with flocks,
and the valleys are decked with grain. They shout in
triumph[H7321]; indeed, they sing.*

Psalm 65:8, 12-13

H7321 *rûwa'*, a primitive root; to mar (especially
by breaking); figuratively, to split the ears (with
sound), i.e. shout (for alarm or joy):—blow an
alarm, cry (alarm, aloud, out), destroy, make
a joyful noise, smart, shout (for joy), sound an
alarm, triumph. (28)

The dawn and the sunset are the Lord's visual shout
of joy to His children to gaze upon and experience a
glimpse of His glory. The meadows are wearing sheep as
clothing, and the fields are ripe with grain—God's provision for all our daily needs. The land shouts for joy in its
service to God. If we present ourselves silent and still before the Lord, we may be able to hear the wind whispering through the grain. The bleating of the sheep is music
to their Creator's ears. If I do not exalt God with every
cell of my being, this psalm declares how His creation is
ready, willing, and capable to take my place.

In what ways can you lift God up by using the gifts and talents He has given you? Finding what the Lord has made you skilled and passionate about and surrendering that back to Him is one way of offering up praise to Him. Be assured God will bless what you have sacrificed back to Him. Another way we praise Him is by purposing to wake up with gratitude as the direction of our life's compass. We need to be grateful that He is upholding us with His righteous right hand (Isaiah 41:10). The Apostle Paul taught that even the earth, not just the people of the earth, is in prison, so to speak (Romans 8:18-25). Even the earth is in its preliminary state, groaning and waiting to be renewed. All evidence of the curse and sin will be burned away, and the New Jerusalem be brought down to the new earth in all its perfection.

Revelation 21:1-2 *Then I saw a new heaven and a new earth for the first heaven and earth had passed away, and the sea was no more. I saw the holy city, the new Jerusalem, coming down out of heaven from God, prepared as a bride adorned for her husband.*

The dawn and sunset shout for joy even while the earth groans waiting to be completely delivered from the effects of humanity's sin. With certain conviction, we can shout for joy even now in this fallen world, knowing that our impending future will be living in the place our forever Bridegroom has prepared for us as the bride of Christ.

Father, may our shouts for joy be almost earsplitting as we praise You for the wonders You have created, Your constant care, and our future in the home prepared for us by Jesus.

Worship along with Darlene Zschech singing "Shout to the Lord:" https://www.youtube.com/watch?v=5_aIauL2xKA

answer

MAKE A JOYFUL NOISE

Make a joyful[H7321] noise to God, all the earth! Sing the glory of His name; make His praise glorious. Say to God, "How awesome are Your deeds! So great is Your power that Your enemies cower before You. All the earth bows down to You; they sing praise to You; they sing praise to Your name." Selah

Come and see the works of God; how awesome are His deeds toward mankind. He turned the sea into dry land; they passed through the waters on foot; there we rejoiced[H8055] in Him.

Psalm 66:1-6

Verse 1 - Make a joyful noise unto God, all ye lands; literally, all the earth - an invitation to the whole world to join in the joy of Israel, wherein they too are interested (comp. Psalm 60:2, 5). Psalm 66:1 (29)

Verse 4 - All peoples of the earth, willingly or unwillingly, will "bow down" before the Lord, singing praise to his holy name. (30)

Philippians 2:9-11 *Therefore God exalted Him to the highest place and gave Him the name above all names, that at the name of Jesus every knee should bow, in heaven and on earth and under the earth, and every tongue confess that Jesus Christ is Lord, to the glory of*

God the Father.

The Israelites testified everywhere they went—many times the story had preceded them—that God led them across the Red Sea on dry land and then drowned Pharoah's army, chariots and horses included, when the sea crashed back over them. This was cause for all the nations—Israelites and Gentiles—to praise God's glory and shout for joy! Even God's enemies would feign obedience and praise to Him because they feared His power. In the future, there will come a day when all the people of the earth will be compelled to declare the Lordship of Jesus Christ and praise God's glory. How much better is it to exalt Him joyfully, sincerely with vitality and fervor now than to be forced to kneel before Him as conquering King and spend eternity in Hell.

We are all eternal beings. The only question is where we will live when our life on earth is over. When it comes to the Lord Jesus, you are either with Him or against Him.

Luke 11:23 *He who is not with Me is against Me, and he who does not gather with Me scatters.*

Have you surrendered your life to Jesus when the Holy Spirit prompted you? When Christ returns to the earth as King, it will be too late. I (Susan) realized at the age of about four or five that I wanted to be on Jesus's team rather than the devil's team. If you are not certain that you have trusted Jesus as your Savior, King, and Lord, we would love to talk with you about your relationship to Him. Contact us at www.preciousjewelsministries.com

Father, we celebrate You with a joyful noise, a shout of triumph because You have delivered us from the power of sin and death. We pray You give us the opportunity to lead others into a saving relationship with You as their Lord that they may join us in making Your praise glorious!

Worship with Sandi Patti singing "Make His Praise Glorious": https://www.youtube.com/watch?v=PoW6U-j6SHNI

Those who live far away fear Your wonders; You make the dawn and sunset shout for joy[H7442].

Psalm 65:8

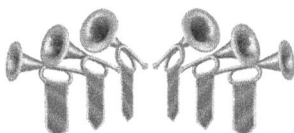

SHOUT FOR JOY!

Shout for joy
> like the golden rays
>> of a glorious dawn.

Shout for joy
> like magenta skies,
>> orange sun just gone.

Shout for joy
> for your many sins
>> He has forgiven.

Shout for joy:
> He's prepared for you
>> a place in Heaven.

Shout for joy!

SONG OF JOY FOR ALL NATIONS

May God be gracious to us and bless us, and cause His face to shine upon us, Selah that Your ways may be known on earth, Your salvation among all nations. Let the peoples praise You, O God; let all the peoples praise You. Let the nations be glad^{H8055} and sing for joy^{H7442}, for You judge the peoples justly and lead the nations of the earth.

Psalm 67:1-4

67:1–7 This brief psalm develops two optimistic themes: the need and result of God's mercy, and the future universal worship of God. The psalm reflects the promise to Abraham that God would bless his descendants, and in Abraham, "all the families of the earth" (Gen. 12:1–3). (31)

This is a futuristic psalm, encouraging all nations to praise God. God's people, the descendants of Abraham and Sarah, were to live so in harmony with God that the Gentiles would be attracted to the God they worshipped. In this way, all nations would be blessed through the Israelites and desire to become proselytes—converts—to the Jewish religion, worshipping the one true God. Jesus's disciples preached salvation first to the Jews and then to the Gentiles. Jesus (Abraham's Seed through whom all nations would be blessed) made it clear that salvation is available to people of all nations

(Matthew 28:19, Mark 16:15).

Galatians 3:16 *The promises were spoken to Abraham and to his seed. The Scripture does not say, "and to seeds," meaning many, but "and to your seed," meaning One, who is Christ.*

Genesis 12:7 (KJV) *And the Lord appeared unto Abram, and said, Unto thy seed will I give this land: and there builded he an altar unto the Lord, who appeared unto him.*

The only ones excluded from God's salvation are those who refuse to believe in and trust Jesus, His Son. He is the righteous judge of all the people groups. This will be completely manifested during the millennial reign of Jesus and forever afterward. When the earth is perfectly ruled by our Lord, it will be peaceful, full of joy, ready to be explored with no fear, and the totality of justice.

I (Susan) am not a singer. My song of praise and joy is found in any way that God communicates to His audience through me, His vessel—teaching, writing, Scripture memes, etc. A visual artist expresses joy through painting, sculpting, etc. A carpenter's joy is found in making wood into something useful and beautiful—a piece of furniture or the framework of a house. For believers, there are many ways to "sing" joyfully to and about our Lord. Each day of our lives should be a joyous melody of praise to the One who gives us strength for each moment. The believer's joy is to live in harmony with the way of the Lord right now. Therefore, when He is ruling and reigning on the earth, we will already be dedicated to this way of living to the point that it is as natural as breathing. We can sing for joy now because we know that God is in control and that ultimately His control will be evident to all. The chaos of the present world does not dissuade us from trust in His control because we know that our security in Christ is guaranteed by His Holy Spirit within us.

Ephesians 1:13-14 *And in Him, having heard and believed the word of truth—the gospel of your salvation—you were sealed with the promised Holy Spirit, who is the pledge of our inheritance until the redemption of those who are God's possession, to the praise of His glory.*

Do you have a song of joy in your heart and on your lips today? Are you confident in the Lord's control? Is your life lived in praise to Jesus, the righteous Judge and Lord of all, by the power of the Holy Spirit within you? You cannot achieve this joy and dedication to the Lord through self-effort. His Holy Spirit enables your obedience, your praise, and your joy. The Spirit empowers us to be instruments in the hands of our Lord.

Father, put a song of joy in our hearts as we trust in Your control over all our circumstances. Help us to sing as joyfully in the darkest days as we do on our best day.

Worship with The Newsboys singing "He Reigns": https://www.youtube.com/watch?v=aKTqwBetI1I

NO LONGER LONELY: JUMPING FOR JOY

But the righteous will be glad[H8055] and rejoice[H5970] be-
fore God; they will celebrate with joy[H7797]. Sing to God!
Sing praises to His name. Exalt Him who rides on the
clouds—His name is the LORD—and rejoice[H5937] before
Him. A father of the fatherless, and a defender of the
widows, is God in His holy habitation. God settles the
lonely in families; He leads the prisoners out to pros-
perity, but the rebellious dwell in a sun-scorched land.

Psalm 68:3-6

H5970 *'âlats,* – a primitive root; to jump for joy,
i.e. exult:—be joyful, rejoice, triumph. (32)

God is a Champion of lonely people, especially those
bereft of nuclear family. He cares for those whose
fathers have died and those whose fathers are absent—
uninvolved—even if they are still in the home. He takes
up the cause of the widows, those whose husbands have
passed away, and we believe those who have been abandoned by husbands, i.e. divorced not by their own choice.
He takes those of us who are single and creates families
for us in atypical ways. Case in point: Susan and I are
a "family" of two. We are not related by blood, but we
are sisters in Christ. We call ourselves "chosen sisters"
or "bonus sisters". God chose to place us in each other's lives, knit our hearts together in His love, move us

in as roommates, and form us into a family so that neither of us would be lonely. We believe we were ordained to remain single to devote ourselves to the Lord as our first Love and priority. God's tender care for those of us who could sulk in the displacement loneliness causes, brought us together to magnify our praise of Him. Susan has never been able to jump physically, but we jump for joy in our hearts! God provides for our every need, even the human need for the companionship of a sister, someone to share our highs and lows, our joys and sadness, our triumphs and our trials. We have the larger "familyship" of all believers, but God knew we needed a special family to share life with daily in our home. Our covenant before God is to live as sisters for the rest of our days.

Are you lonely? God is with you always, but if you need a person with skin on to be with you, ask Him to provide for that need. However, be prepared for the fact that it might be a brother or sister or a child who needs a godly influence rather than a husband or wife. Singleness is not a curse or a demotion. In fact, it can be a great blessing when used to bring glory to God if He has given you the ability to remain single.

1 Corinthians 7:32-34 *I want you to be free from concern. The unmarried man is concerned about the work of the Lord, how he can please the Lord. But the married man is concerned about the affairs of this world, how he can please his wife, and his interests are divid-*

ed. The unmarried woman or virgin is concerned about the work of the Lord, how she can be holy in both body and spirit. But the married woman is concerned about the affairs of this world, how she can please her husband.

Again, seek the Lord concerning marriage and trust Him to direct you. Our prayer as young women was, "Lord if there is someone out there with whom I can serve You better, show him to me. If not, then give me the grace to serve you wholeheartedly in my singleness."

Father, we thank You that even though You chose for us to be unmarried, You gave us each other as bonus sisters. You have shown us we can serve You faithfully and effectively by working together in ministry and sharing a home as chosen family.

Whitney Houston and CeCe Winans singing "Count on Me". Susie and I sing this to each other as sister/friends (Proverbs 18:24b): https://www.youtube.com/watch?v=hgXEnogKXUo

EXPLOSIVE PRAISE

So I will praise You with the harp for Your faithfulness,
O my God; I will sing praise to You with the lyre, O
Holy One of Israel. When I sing praise to You, my lips
will shout for joy[H7442], along with my soul, which You
have redeemed. My tongue will indeed proclaim Your
righteousness all day long, for those who seek my harm
are disgraced and confounded.

Psalm 71:22-24

God is trustworthy, and no matter what we are going through, our gifts and our propensities remain. In the midst of the trial or challenge, we must continue to praise Him and not allow the difficulties to define us or cause us to move away from our God-given purpose, our divine assignment. Our response to an awesome and perfect God needs to be exalting, explosive praise. Even though He is high above our human existence, our Heavenly Father stoops down to lift us up in order to have relationship with Him and thus to be raised into heavenly places with Him. Our lips should embrace praise continuously for God's watchful eye is ever present in our joy and in our troubles.

Here is a short list of some of the trials God has brought me, Susan, through. Keep in mind that even though I have these challenges, they do not have a hold on me.

- Born prematurely, 10 weeks early, in 1966

- "Died" at least twice during birth/delivery
- Cerebral Palsy affecting all four limbs (life expectancy 24 years, but God has brought me to 57 years as of 2023)
- Eye surgeries beginning at three years old
- Scoliosis surgery at 15 years old (spinal curvature of 98° corrected to 35° with over 300 stitches, removal of three ribs, and deflating and reinflating my left lung)
- Multiple orthopedic surgeries between 6 and 16 years old
- Sixteen lithotripsies in a two-and-a-half-year period as an adult
- Left nephrectomy (removal of kidney) in November 2010
- Severe sleep apnea (my brain forgets to breathe)
- Bilateral amputation of legs above the knee in August 2015

Take a few moments to make a list of the times God has brought you through struggles. Remembering and seeing God's faithfulness in print will enable you to remain built up in the middle of the next trial and face it with faith and courage. This will give you cause to shout out explosive, joyful praise instantaneously!

Father, I (Susie) tend to be a quiet, contemplative worshiper, but getting to understand all You have carried Susan through to make her into the faith-filled, joy-

JOY: Blossoms among the Thorns

ous, delightful bonus sister You have blessed me with, makes me want to explode with shouts of joy! May we always focus on the way You are helping us be over-comers rather than be overwhelmed by our challenges!

STRIKE UP THE HOLY SPIRIT BAND

Sing for joy[H7442] to God our strength; make a joyful[H7321] noise to the God of Jacob. Lift up a song, strike the tambourine, play the sweet-sounding harp and lyre.

Psalm 81:1-2

The preamble of this psalm is a call to worship. Often, we come to worship reactively because it is expected of us instead of choosing a spirit of joy beforehand. Why does the psalmist exclaim joyfully? God is his energy, his vitality, and his vibrancy. Because God is our strength, we can use every instrument that makes a sound to praise Him: voices, pianos, guitars, drums, trumpets, clarinets, flutes, tambourines, etc. There was a member of the church where we worship who, due to cerebral palsy, was "non-verbal." However, when the choir and/or the instruments would lift up praise to the Lord, he would lift up his voice in a joyful shout. The congregation could not understand his words, but they could sense the praise in his heart as he worshipped his Lord; and God understood his praises perfectly. Now in Heaven, Darrell Zimmerman is praising His Lord with the joyous words his earth-suit prevented him from using when he lived among us. In our flesh and self-effort, we are weak; but when everything we are—our entire being—is submitted to and released to God, the strength we depend upon is God's and God's alone. And His strength will never fail us as we endeavor to fulfill His purposes for our lives.

For further insight into God's strength through you, look up the following verses: Psalm 28:7, Isaiah 40:9, 2 Corinthians 12:9, Ephesians 3:16, Colossians 1:11, 2 Thessalonians 3:3 and one of our favorites:

Philippians 4:13 (AMP) *I can do all things [which He has called me to do] through Him who strengthens and empowers me [to fulfill His purpose—I am self-sufficient in Christ's sufficiency; I am ready for anything and equal to anything through Him who infuses me with inner strength and confident peace.]*

A band is a group of musicians working toward the common goal of making music with various instruments and/or voices. When you worship with your local congregation this week, think of yourself as a part of a "Holy Spirit Band". Together, filled with the Holy Spirit, you will play and sing joyfully to the praise and glory of our Lord. The people on the platform are the lead worshipers, but each worshiper (including you!) is an important part of the ensemble.

Father, may we march to the beat of the Holy Spirit praising You joyfully every day! May we care less about what others think of our ability to play or sing and more about how much our "joyful noise" is music to our Lord's ears!

Sing along with Russ Taff on "Trumpet of Jesus".
https://www.youtube.com/watch?v=XnsPvNbjo-8

HEART'S SONG

How lovely is Your dwelling place, O LORD of Hosts! My soul longs, even faints, for the courts of the LORD; my heart and my flesh cry out[H7442] for the living God.

Psalm 84:1-2

How lovely is your dwelling place, O Lord of hosts! My soul longs, yes, faints for the courts of the Lord; my heart and flesh sing for joy[H7442] to the living God.

Psalm 84:1-2 (ESV)

If someone opens the door of their home to you, you enter and say, "How nice to see you! Your home is so beautiful!" For Jesus's home, I'm not sure we will really have words because we will be overwhelmed by the opulence of it all. I think we will be speechless. My heart aches in anticipation of being with the Lord forever. People see the more obvious limitations caused by my cerebral palsy, but not walking and not always having complete control of my arms are not the most frustrating challenges. There are others. I must have assistance with eating. I can manage finger foods, such as tater tots and chocolate almonds if they are laid on my chest, but Susie helps me with the rest of my meals. If I need my spectaculars—my name for my glasses—someone has to place them on my face, so I often leave them on at night in case I wake up and want to watch television. That way, I don't have to wake someone up. I cannot grab my own tissue when I have a cold. I am unable to transfer from the bed to my wheelchair without the assistance of TWO people. Susie cannot use a lift to move me because I have two long metal rods in my back due to surgery to correct scoliosis. However, in the middle of all these things, the Lord purposed me to be His megaphone to proclaim His gospel message. My heart cries out, sings for joy, in praise of the living God. Susie says my heart sings "Frosty the Snowman" because it goes "thumpity-thump-thump". She was a music major, so she should know. LOL. In reality, my spirit, body, and heart declare with melody and gladness that my Savior lives.

I'm sure you have difficulties in this life as well. Reflect on your future home in Heaven. Doesn't it make even your cells dance for joy? Your heart can sing even on the worst days if you keep your focus on Jesus, all He's done and will do for you!

Father, may our heart's song always be a praise medley proclaiming the greatness of our Lord. It matters not to You whether we can carry a tune in a bucket. What matters most is the attitude of our heart and that our gaze is fixed upon Jesus. Take our minds off our struggles and help them dwell on our future home with You!

Worship along with Kutless singing "Better is One Day": https://www.youtube.com/watch?v=jdEo3zRJtxw

SPRINGS OF JOY
FLOW FROM OUR FATHER

Singers and pipers will proclaim, "All my springs of joy[H4599] are in You."

Psalm 87:7

87:1–7 This psalm describes the Lord's love for Jerusalem and exalts this city as the religious center of the world in the coming messianic kingdom (cf. Ps. 48). Though the nations of the world (even including some of Israel's former enemies) will worship the Lord then, Israel will still be the favored nation (cf. Is. 2:2–4; 19:23–25; 45:22–25; 56:6–8; Zech. 8:20–23; 14:16–19). (33)

87:7 "All my springs are in you." "Springs" is a metaphor for the source of joyful blessings. Eternal salvation, including the death and resurrection of Christ, is rooted in Jerusalem. The prophets also tell of a literal fountain flowing from the temple in Jerusalem which will water the surrounding land (cf. Joel 3:18; Ezek. 47:1–12). (34)

We are blessed because we are the children of God. We have placed our trust in the death, burial, and resurrection of Jesus who purchased our salvation on the cross in Jerusalem. Every grace-filled gift—blessing—begins and ends with God.

James 1:17 *Every good and perfect gift is from above, coming down from the Father of the heavenly lights, with whom there is no change or shifting shadow.*

I am thankful the Lord blessed me with the ability to speak. After experiencing double amputation above the knee and surviving a "Code Blue" being called on my behalf, I am thankful to be alive! I am blessed to have a facilitator—"Tater" for short—my roommate, Susie, who has become my bonus sister and partner in ministry. I am thankful for loving grandparents who took me to church as a child. I am thankful for a mom who takes pleasure in me. We are blessed that the Lord enabled us to become a non-profit corporation, 501(C)3 and to develop our website, www.preciousjewelsministries.com. I am blessed by chicken fried steak with gravy and chocolate, but not together! EVERY good thing in our lives is God's gift. In light of this awesome truth that all blessings flow like a spring from God, we need to express paramount gratitude and thanksgiving to the Lord.

Make your own list of things for which you are grateful to God——the blessings flowing from your Father. Lift up a prayer of thanksgiving and joy, acknowledging that your Father has showered you with extravagant love.

Father, we thank You that blessings continue to flow, to spring up in our lives as we follow You. Thank You that each new day is a gift from You that holds numerous blessings if we open our eyes to see them.

Worship with this hymn "Open My Eyes that I May See" by the Joslin Grove Choral Society : https://www.you-tube.com/watch?v=GDceaG7kFQA

CELEBRATE YOUR BLESSINGS WITH A JOYFUL SHOUT!

Blessed are those who know the joyful[H8643] sound, who walk, O LORD, in the light of Your presence. They rejoice[H1523] in Your name all day long, and in Your righteousness they exult. For You are the glory of their strength, and by Your favor our horn is exalted.

Psalm 89:15-17

Even though the latter part of the Psalm is a lament over the seeming end of the Davidic Dynasty, the psalmist knows and trusts that God promised an obedient King from David's lineage would rule and reign forever. We know this King to be Jesus Christ. Even though the psalmist lived before the fulfillment of God's promise through Jesus, he still exulted in God's blessings to Israel and all who rejoice in His name; and he believed God would keep His promise to David. Jewish festivals began with trumpet blasts and joyful shouts. The worshippers celebrated God who had chosen them to be His people. God has chosen those of us who follow Jesus to be His people, His adopted children. He has blessed us with every spiritual blessing (Ephesians 1:3). Do we shout joyfully because of the privilege of walking in God's presence? Do we rejoice at the sound of the name Jesus? Or do we get more excited about sporting events or Hollywood entertainers? Do we celebrate His righteousness that He has graciously credited to our account? Or are we so beaten down by the mundaneness of daily life, that we cease to see our blessings? Let us get less dragged down by the daily challenges and more revved up by the promises and the faithful provision of our Heavenly Father.

Take a few minutes to count your blessings once again. Perhaps you could even write them down in a journal or, as was suggested to us, put them on strips of paper and keep them in a blessing jar. Then you can pull some out to be reminded of God's faithfulness when things seem to be going awry. After dwelling on the good gifts your Father has bestowed on you, give a joyful shout. It's okay to shout in your house. It might even be okay to shout in God's house next Sunday!

Father, help us to go to sleep counting our blessings rather than worrying about tomorrow. Help us rejoice in You!

Some good reminders in song: Bing Crosby and Rosemary Clooney singing "Count Your Blessings": https://www.youtube.com/watch?v=DXKxazgio2s

Or Guy Penrod singing "Count Your Blessings, Name Them One by One": https://www.youtube.com/watch?v=9o0jWVSWS3M

MAKE US GLAD, LORD

Satisfy us in the morning with Your loving devotion[H2617],
that we may sing for joy[H7442] and be glad[H8055] all our
days. Make us glad[H8055] for as many days as You have
afflicted us, for as many years as we have seen evil.

Psalm 90:14-15
(a prayer of Moses the man of God)

90:1–17 The thrust of this magnificent prayer is
to ask God to have mercy on frail human beings
living in a sin-cursed universe. Moses begins the
psalm with a reflection on God's eternality, then
expresses his somber thoughts about the sor-
rows and brevity of life in their relationship to
God's anger, and concludes with a plea that God
would enable His people to live a significant life.
The psalm seems to have been composed as the
older generation of Israelites who had left Egypt
were dying off in the wilderness (Num. 14). (35)

H2617 cheçed – a masculine noun indicating
kindness, loving-kindness, mercy, goodness,
faithfulness, love, acts of kindness . . . The clas-
sic text for understanding the significance of this
word is Psalm 136 where it is used twenty-six
times to proclaim that God's kindness and love
are eternal. (36)

Moses prayed for God's chosen people, the Israelites. His petition was that after the long night of affliction and trials, they would see a new dawn of God's loving-kindness. He prays that the days of joy would equal the days of their affliction. Moses is certain the response to God's comfort, relief, and mercy toward the Israelites will result in songs of joy and gladness the rest of their days. Only God can create gladness in the shadow of sadness. Sometimes He does it through people sharing just the right words. Sometimes when you feel so low you could play handball against the curb (slightly shorter than me LOL), God can elevate your mood with a baby's laughter. I've been in such chronic sudden pain that I have screamed out the name of the Lord in the middle of the night. Sometimes it feels like days of affliction will never end, when the temporary of this life seems to be awfully permanent. But then God sends the dawn of joy. I've never had the fun of feeling the breeze in my hair while running or riding a bike, but when the Holy Spirit is flowing through me as I study or teach God's word, I feel that freedom. When I listen to "The Hallelujah Chorus" and wave my hand like a conductor to express my worship, I feel the joy of God's loving-kindness.

Are you feeling depressed, afflicted? Are you experiencing chronic pain or financial struggles? Pray. Ask the Lord to send a new dawn of His loving-kindness to you and to fill you with His joy because His loving-kindness, peace, and joy are everlasting. Remember that the trials of this life are fleeting compared with the glory we will experience in His presence forever!

Romans 8:18 (AMPC) *For I consider that the sufferings of this present time (this present life) are not worth being compared with the glory that is about to be revealed to us and in us and for us and conferred on us!*

Father, we thank You for the breezes of joy that flow over us even as we struggle with pain, sorrow, or trials. We pray for the day You grant us complete healing and joy unspeakable and unending, and we trust Your wisdom as to when that comes.

Worship while listening to this instrumental version of "The Hallelujah Chorus." Maybe even pretend to conduct it!
https://www.youtube.com/watch?v=1XqRXG8NxMw

DAILY SONGS OF JOY:
I CHOOSE TO SING!

It is good to praise the LORD, and to sing praises to Your name, O Most High, to proclaim Your loving devotion in the morning and Your faithfulness at night with the ten-stringed harp and the melody of the lyre. For You, O LORD, have made me glad[H8055] by Your deeds; I sing for joy[H7422] at the works of Your hands. How great are Your works, O LORD, how deep are Your thoughts!
Psalm 92:1-5 (a song for the Sabbath day)

God's loving devotion, faithfulness, and mighty deeds are all reasons to praise His name joyfully with singing and playing of instruments. However, being in an attitude of praise all day long no matter what is happening within or without is easier said than done even just for our day of worship. Praise and rejoicing should be a daily practice or lifestyle of the believer rather than something we muster up on the Lord's Day. By Sunday, we should all be so filled with the Holy Spirit from remembering God's loving devotion, faithfulness, and mighty works in our lives all week that the church building becomes a "filling station" for those who are going through a rough time. Our joy in the Lord should flow freely so that others can drink it in and be reinvigorated to praise the Lord themselves. Verses 12-15 of Psalm 92 talk of those who follow the Lord being like an evergreen tree, "full of sap" in the Amplified Version. The way to remain full of vigor into old age is to practice what these first five verses of the Psalm tell us is "good." Every day, we need to proclaim God's love and faithfulness and remind ourselves not only of His mighty deeds recorded in the Bible but those seen in our own lives on a day-to-day basis.

Try beginning each morning with a prayer of praise for the Father's love rather than just petitioning Him for what He can do for you. Try ending each day remembering God's faithfulness and His answers to your prayers, His works in your life. Remember that you yourself are "God's workmanship, created in Christ Jesus to do good works, which God prepared in advance as our way of life" (Ephesians 2:10). You may want to try keeping a journal of answered prayer or works of God in your life that you can pull out when it is difficult to see His love and faithfulness during a rough time.

Father, we praise You for Your unfailing love for us even when we fall short of Your desires for us. We praise Your faithfulness that never fails even though we fail to recognize it at times. We thank You, Lord, for the many ways You have worked in and through our lives to bring glory to Your name.

Worship by listening or singing along with Paul Baloche's song "Psalm 92 (Oh Most High)":
https://www.youtube.com/watch?v=jERlH2pg7e4

ROCK CONCERT

Come, let us sing for joy[H7442] to the LORD; let us shout[H7321] to the Rock of our salvation! Let us enter His presence with thanksgiving; let us make a joyful noise[H7321] to Him in song.

Psalm 95:1-2

God, who is the Rock, provided water from the Rock. Numbers 20:8 states, "Take the staff and assemble the congregation. You and your brother Aaron are to speak to the rock while they watch, and it will pour out its water. You will bring out water from the rock and provide drink for the congregation and their livestock." According to 1 Corinthians 10:3-4, Jesus was the Rock that poured out the water, "They all ate the same spiritual food and drank the same spiritual drink; for they drank from the spiritual rock that accompanied them, and that rock was Christ." Jesus, being the Rock, is the provision and is the River of Life. John 7:38 says, "Whoever believes in Me, as the Scripture has said: 'Streams of living water will flow from within him.'" The living water is the Holy Spirit flowing through the life of the believer and bearing witness to the world. The Rock, in Scripture, is also a symbol of safety and security. The high rocks of the holy land served as natural fortresses. Jesus is our stronghold, and we rest safely in His care.

I had only known Susan for eleven months, when I stayed in the hospital with her through major surgery.

She had come through the bilateral above-the-knee amputation surgery well and was getting settled in a regular hospital room for the night. I had not really eaten since noon, and it was now nearing midnight. While the respiratory therapist was trying to get her oxygen adjusted, I ran down to the cafeteria. I came back to the room, ate two bites of my pizza, and realized Susan's oxygen saturation was too low according to the monitor. The respiratory therapist and the nurse came in to try to replace the nasal cannula with a face mask. I kept telling Susan to breathe. Suddenly the nurse hit the big, red button on the wall and called "Code Blue." Susan had ceased breathing at all! I exclaimed, "Susan, I am not leaving you! I will be in the hallway." She says she was aware of my promise even as they were sitting astraddle her and "bagging" her to squeeze air into her lungs. I sank against the wall in the hallway for fear I would fall, but as I began saying the Lord's prayer (couldn't formulate a prayer of my own at that moment), I realized it was not the wall I was leaning on but the Rock, our Lord Jesus Christ. He faithfully held me up!

Do you remember a time when you had to lean heavily on Christ the solid Rock? Let us sing and shout joyfully to the Rock. Let's hold a "Rock" concert!

Father, we thank You that we have a solid foundation, a strong Rock, on which to place our faith. Thank You for the many times You have held us up when we thought our knees might buckle. May we sing in worship to the Rock of our salvation all our days!

Worship with Psalm 95 set to music by John Michael Talbot:
https://www.youtube.com/watch?v=-_h8hvqpfVo

Or sing "Jesus is the Rock and He Rolls My Blues Away" with Phil Driscol: https://www.youtube.com/watch?v=9wTbPrSWOqM

HEAVENS AND EARTH REJOICE

Let the heavens be glad [H8055] *and the earth rejoice;* [H1523]
let the sea resound, and all that fills it. Let the fields ex-
ult [H5937], *and all that is in them. Then all the trees of the*
forest will sing for joy [H7442] *before the LORD, for He is*
coming—He is coming to judge the earth. He will judge
the world in righteousness and the peoples in His faith-
fulness.

> *Psalm 96:11-13 (See also 1 Chronicles 15 & 16)*

David composed this Psalm for the celebration of bringing the Ark of the Covenant into Jerusalem from the house of Obed-edom:

1 Chronicles 16:7 *On that day David first committed to Asaph and his brothers this song of thanksgiving to the LORD.*

Another section of this song is recorded in Psalm 105. When the Ark of the Covenant was installed in the tent David had prepared for it, this song was sung to the accompaniment of harps, lyres, cymbals, and trumpets. David wrote that even the heavens and earth, and all that is in them, rejoice because of the greatness of God. Their joy cannot be contained. The King James Version says the "seas roar!" This Psalm looks forward to the righteous rule of the Messiah when He returns as the Righteous Judge.

96:13 He is coming. The rule of the Lord described in this psalm is not the present universal kingdom (Ps. 93), but one which will be established when Christ returns to earth. (37)

For those of us who have trusted Jesus for salvation and eternal life, judgement is not to be feared because we are covered in Christ's righteousness and not dependent on our own ability to be good enough. All evil will be extinguished, and the Lord Jesus will reign in righteousness and faithfulness over everything. This will definitely be a time to rejoice!

We can have joy even in this present world with all its woes because we know that ultimately Jesus wins, Satan is defeated, and we will live in perfect peace forever! As CeCe Winans sings, "Don't have to wait 'til the battle's over. We can shout now!"

Don't let the heavens, earth, seas, fields, and trees outdo you in praising the Lord. Express your joy and thanksgiving to God even now! Maybe even sing along with Cece:
https://www.youtube.com/watch?v=WzBCn4Js8kA

Father, we thank You that our joy does not depend on our current circumstances but depends entirely on Your faithfulness to us as Your chosen children.

REJOICE IN GOD'S POWER TO PRESERVE

The LORD reigns, let the earth rejoice;[H1523] let the distant shores be glad[H8055]. . .

Hate evil, O you who love the LORD! He preserves the souls of His saints; He delivers them from the hand of the wicked. Light shines on the righteous, gladness[H8057] on the upright in heart. Rejoice[H8055] in the LORD, you righteous ones, and praise His holy name.

Psalm 97:1, 10-12

This could be a song for the coronation of Jesus as the King of kings and Lord of lords. Those of us who are Christ-followers—who have surrendered our lives to Jesus as Sovereign over all— should abhor evil because He is holy, perfectly righteous. As our all-powerful King, Jesus delivers us from evil and preserves our souls. Jesus even included a plea for this help in His example prayer:

Matthew 6:13 *And lead us not into temptation, but deliver us from the evil one.*

We take joy in knowing that we are not responsible for keeping ourselves in God's favor. We can never earn or deserve the privilege of being His children. We are only righteous in His eyes because the Father sees the righteousness of Jesus covering us. Once we belong to the Lord by trusting Jesus, we can never lose our position as an adopted child of God. God completes His work in us (Philippians 1:6), no one can snatch us out of His hand (John 10:27-30), and He will enable us to stand (Romans 14:4):

Philippians 1:6 *being confident of this, that He who began a good work in you will carry it on to completion until the day of Christ Jesus.*

John 10:27-30 *"My sheep listen to My voice; I know them, and they follow Me. I give them eternal life, and they will never perish. No one can snatch them out of My hand. My Father who has given them to Me is greater than all. No one can snatch them out of My Father's hand. I and the Father are one."*

Romans 14:4 *Who are you to judge someone else's servant? To his own master he stands or falls. And he will stand, for the Lord is able to make him stand.*

Joyfully celebrate with confidence that God's got you and will never let you go! When life's struggles seem to pile up on you, it can be a challenge to remember; but our God is the faithful and powerful King and will preserve His precious jewels—His children.

Father, You rule over everything, and You have the power to preserve us, Your saints, through the trials of this earth. We have joy knowing we will eventually live with You in perfect peace, love, and joy!

Here's a song to remind you that the Lord Reigns by Dennis Jernigan: https://www.youtube.com/watch?v=CPYUe451CKA

ERUPTION OF JOYFUL PRAISES

Make a joyful[H7321] noise to the LORD, all the earth;
break forth—let your cry ring out, and sing praises!
Sing praises to the LORD with the lyre, in melodious
song with the harp. With trumpets and the blast of the
ram's horn shout for joy[H7321] before the LORD, the King.

Psalm 98:4-6

> 98:4 Shout joyfully. A great cheer, greeting and
> welcoming a king (cf. Zech. 9:9; Matt. 21:4–9).
> Break forth. The idea is that of an eruption of
> praise which could not be contained (cf. Is. 14:7;
> 44:23; 55:12). (38)

All the people and the earth itself erupt in praise at the coming of the great King. The instruments used to accompany the joyful singing are used in temple worship which indicates these cheers—these shouts of joy—are for the Lord Himself, the King of kings. Imagine the praises welling up inside the people until they could not be contained, bursting forth in a volcanic crescendo of joy! Perhaps this is the kind of praise Handel was trying to express as he composed the "Hallelujah Chorus." We read an interesting article about the tradition of standing when the "Hallelujah Chorus" is sung or played. The tradition began because of the king of England's response at the very first performance of Handel's Messiah.

King George II stood up at the performance of George Frederick Handel's "Hallelujah chorus" on March 23,

1743. Read the entire article here: https://romanroad-spress.com/2016/12/why-the-king-stood/

Was the king of England simply caught up in the emotion of a great musical work, or as a Christian, was he standing in honor of a King far greater than himself. Since he never explained his gesture, we will never know for sure. However, we agree with the author of the article mentioned above that we should stand in honor of the King of kings when His presence is announced!

Susie admits to having been reserved in her worship for much of her life. However, she is learning to embrace exuberant joy in the Lord. Do you tend to hold back when praising the Lord? Our Lord is a victorious warrior! He is our defender and deliverer. We are to make a joyful NOISE and SHOUT for joy! Do not be afraid to open up and express the joy you have found because you enjoy a relationship with the Almighty! Don't hold back. ERUPT in joyful praise!

Father, we know there are times for reverence and quiet awe, but we also see there are times that require a volcanic crescendo of joy! Help us to not be shy about expressing the joy that fills us because of Your presence in our lives.

Worship while listening to or singing along with "The Hallelujah Chorus." https://www.youtube.com/watch?v=9jvsK798Lbs

(Yes, we included this piece twice, without and with voices.)

JOYFUL SHEEP

Make a joyful[H7321] noise to the LORD, Serve the LORD with gladness;[8057] come into His presence with joyful[H7445] songs. Know that the LORD is God. It is He who made us, and we are His; we are His people, and the sheep of His pasture. Enter His gates with thanksgiving and His courts with praise; give thanks to Him and bless His name. For the LORD is good, and His loving devotion endures forever; His faithfulness continues to all generations.

Psalm 100:1-5

The Bible compares God's people to sheep in many places. We found a good article that delineates exactly how people are like sheep here: https://momremade.com/god-compares-us-to-sheep/

The importance of the psalmist's reference to sheep in Psalm 100 is that we are the Lord's sheep and belong in His pasture.

Psalm 23:1 *The LORD is my shepherd; I shall not want.*

Isaiah 53:6 *We all like sheep have gone astray, each one has turned to his own way; and the LORD has laid upon Him the iniquity of us all.*

Ezekiel 34:31 *'You are My flock, the sheep of My pasture, My people, and I am your God,' declares the Lord GOD."*

John 10:27 *My sheep hear My voice, and I know them, and they follow Me.*

1 Peter 2:25 *For "you were like sheep going astray," but now you have returned to the Shepherd and Overseer of your souls.*

Why are the Lord's sheep joyful? He is both provider and protector of the sheep. We have all that we need, and our thirst for righteousness is quenched by His Holy Spirit (Matthew 5:6). He guards our lives like the shepherd who literally lies down as the door to the sheep fold. When we listen for our Shepherd's voice we are guided in the right way. Left to our own devices, we stray away from the path, get hurt, or fall down. But our Good Shepherd pursues us when we wander from the safety of the fold. We are joyful sheep when we entrust our welfare to the One who created us, called us, redeemed us, and is making us more and more like Himself.

Matthew 18:12 *What do you think? If a man has a hundred sheep and one of them goes astray, will he not leave the ninety-nine on the hills and go out to search for the one that is lost?*

John 10:11 *I am the good shepherd. The good shepherd lays down His life for the sheep.*

Have you become a disgruntled sheep? Sheep are most secure in the presence of the Shepherd. Are you listening for the voice of Jesus? Sheep are happiest when they are with the flock. Are you making time to fellowship with other sheep (Christ-followers)? If a sheep falls on its back, it cannot get up without help. Are you struggling to get back on your feet instead of asking the Good Shepherd to help you? Stay in the flock. Stay close to the Shepherd. Seek the help of God and His people when you need it. Return to the joy of being a sheep belonging to the Good Shepherd.

Father, help us to remember to listen for and follow the voice of our own Shepherd, Jesus Christ. Help us to flock together with His other sheep to help each other stay safe. Help us to feed on Your word as nourishment for our souls. Help us to be joyful!

Dennis Jernigan wrote "I Am a Sheep" as a lullaby for his children, but it is a good reminder for adults as well: https://www.youtube.com/watch?v=KEvhGuxOGgo

I will sing to the LORD all my life; I will sing praise to my God while I have my being. May my meditation be pleasing to Him, for I rejoice in the LORD.

Psalm 104:33-34

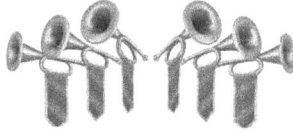

MEDITATING MINSTREL

Father, focus my meditation on You
and give me understanding from Your word.
Let my songs continually praise You
and draw others to You as Lord.
I rejoice that You desire to have
communication with me.
Praise the Lord, O my soul!
God help me to clearly see
Your glory that endures forever,
the many works of Your hands.
You are Creator, Sustainer of all the earth,
and my Father who understands.

OUT OF SIN INTO SALVATION'S JOY

For he remembered his sacred promise to his servant Abraham. So he brought his people out of Egypt with joy[H8342], his chosen ones with rejoicing[H7440]. He gave his people the lands of pagan nations, and they harvested crops that others had planted. All this happened so they would follow his decrees and obey his instructions. Praise the Lord!

Psalm 105:42-45 (NLT)

105:42–45 The psalmist concludes with a summary that alludes to Joshua's leading the nation back into the Land, first promised to Abraham, (Josh. 1–12) and then distributed to the 12 tribes of Israel (Josh. 13–24). What God promised (cf. 105:7–12) He delivered. (39)

105:45 What was the reason for the Lord's remarkable deeds on behalf of Israel? That they might keep his statutes and obey his instructions. Similarly, God saves us so that we will love and obey him. We are not delivered from sin and death so that we can go our own way. We are rescued for reverence; we are saved to serve. (40)

In the first 41 verses of Psalm 105, David recounts how the Lord delivered His chosen people Israel from slavery in Egypt by sending plagues until Pharoah released them. He tells them to remember the wondrous deeds of their God and tell people about them. He reminds them how God provided manna and quail in the wilderness for four decades and preserved them as they journeyed to the land promised to their forefather Abraham. Then he recalls how God brought them out of Egypt and into Canaan with shouts of joy. The bottom line is that God was creating a nation that would honor and obey Him and be a light to the world. The Israelites were to be a blessing to all the nations:

Genesis 18:18 *Abraham will surely become a great and powerful nation, and through him all the nations of the earth will be blessed.*

Ultimately, that blessing would come through "Jesus, the son of David, the son of Abraham" (Matthew 1:1). When we trust in Jesus's finished work on the cross, we are grafted—adopted—into God's family. Christians, those who follow Christ, have also been chosen by God to serve Him, obey Him, and share His light to others. We, too, have been brought from our slavery to sin into the everlasting light of Jesus:

1 Peter 2:9 *But you are a chosen people, a royal priesthood, a holy nation, a people for God's own possession, to proclaim the virtues of Him who called you out of darkness into His marvelous light.*

We should shout for joy! Like Israel, God has called us out for His purpose. We are to share His message—the Good News of His grace—within the sphere of our influence. We do not earn the privilege of being in His family by good deeds. However, once His Holy Spirit inhabits us, we will do the good things He has designed for us to do.

Ephesians 2:8-10 *For it is by grace you have been saved through faith, and this not from yourselves; it is the gift of God, not by works, so that no one can boast. For we are God's workmanship, created in Christ Jesus to do good works, which God prepared in advance as our way of life.*

Father, may we live with gratitude and joy. May remembering where we came from and how You have delivered us make us want to shout with joy as we are led by the Spirit to do Your will.

Worship with the Bangalore Men's Ensemble singing a song Susie has loved since childhood: "Make Me a Blessing."
https://www.youtube.com/watch?v=YSEThVEhw3Q

BARREN NO MORE

He settles the barren woman in her home as a joyful[H8056]
mother to her children. Hallelujah!

Psalm 113:9

Think about the barren women in the Bible. Sarah conceived in her old age and gave birth to the child through whom all nations would be blessed. Rachel's sister outdid her in the giving birth category, but when the Lord opened Rachel's womb, he blessed her with Joseph who would save his people from famine. Hannah prayed for a son and promised to give him back to the Lord, and Samuel became the last judge and a prophet who would anoint Israel's first and second kings. Ruth thought she might never have children not due to her own barrenness but because her husband died, leaving her childless. God provided the kinsman-redeemer Boaz, and she gave birth to the grandfather of King David. God directed Samuel to choose David as Saul's successor. Elizabeth was barren, and like Sarah, was too old to conceive. However, the Lord opened her womb, and she gave birth to John the Baptist, the one who would prepare the way of the Lord!

There are many ways God can create a family. Paul called Timothy his "son in the faith." Susan has no children of her own, but she has numerous goddaughters and one godson, the lone prince. The traditional means of having children was not God's plan for her, but God chose another way to minister to her need to nurture others. God brought godchildren into her life to fulfill her mother's heart. Joy comes through relinquishing our own plans and accepting God's far superior plan. Susie was "adopted" by children she served as a nanny during their teenage years. She, too, had been single and childless, and at one point she felt God gave her the verse above as a promise. It was not fulfilled until she was forty years old, but that was God's perfect timing to bless both her and the children she came to love. God can miraculously open a woman's womb as He did for those women in the paragraph above. We have a dear friend who has been blessed with three children after six miscarriages. She is definitely a joyful mother of children!

Perhaps you are feeling "barren," not literally but in your usefulness to the Lord. We both felt "barren" as far as using our gifts for God's glory and kingdom until He brought us together to work as His team. Keep praying! When He does give you a mission, obey Him, and be prepared for Him to do great things! God is the source of joy. He is the source of life. He is the source of purpose. He is the source of all good things! If you feel like there is anything of import missing in your life whether it be children, a job, a spouse, a ministry, or whatever, seek the Lord in anticipation of His perfect provision for your life.

Father, thank You for fulfilling our need to nurture people even as we are nurturing each other. Thank You for helping us to see that we could serve You better togeth-er than each of us could alone. We are learning to trust Your timing and Your way of answering our prayers.

REJOICING IN THE RULES?!

I rejoice[H7797] in the way of Your testimonies as much as in all riches.

Psalm 119:14

"Testimonies" can also be translated decrees, laws, rules, or instructions. How many children do you know who REJOICE because of their parents' rules? As adults we realize all the rules and instructions, the "laying down of the law" in our childhood homes was for our own good, but we sure could not see it at the time. Children are convinced curfews and limitations are meant to keep them from having fun; but their parents are attempting to keep them safe in a dangerous, fallen world. The same is true for the rules the Lord has set forth for us in the Bible. They are designed to help us navigate this world by sticking to the path He has chosen for us, the path that keeps us in constant "familyship" with Jesus, our best Friend. Jesus Himself said, "Greater love has no one than this, that he lay down his life for his friends. You are My friends if you do what I command you." (John 15:13-14). In Psalm 119:1, we learned that we are to "walk in the light" which is reinforced by 1 John 1:7, "But if we walk in the light as He is in the light, we have fellowship with one another, and the blood of Jesus His Son cleanses us from all sin." When we realize that the commands in God's word help us to walk in the light, and walking in the light deepens our relationship with Jesus and fellow believers, then we can truly rejoice in God's rules. Jesus is the Captain of the Host, the Lord of God's armies:

Joshua 5:13-15 *Now when Joshua was near Jericho, he looked up and saw a man standing in front of him with a drawn sword in His hand. Joshua approached Him and asked, "Are You for us or for our enemies?" "Neither," He replied. "I have now come as Commander of the LORD's army." Then Joshua fell facedown in reverence and asked Him, "What does my Lord have to say to His servant?" The Commander of the LORD's army replied, "Take off your sandals, for the place where you are standing is holy." And Joshua did so.*

He commands us, and we need to obey immediately like Joshua did. When we truly see the value of God's word, His instructions, we will treasure it more than any earthly riches. Adults who had loving parents treasure the instructions they were given as children because they now understand the intent was to protect them rather than annoy them. Mature believers are thankful for the commands found in the Bible because we know God uses them to guide us.

Is there any area of your life that you know is in conflict with the word of God? If so, confess it as sin, and ask the Lord to cleanse you. Do not resist God's rules and ways. Instead learn to rely on them and rejoice in them.

Father, help us to treasure Your rules rather than to rebel against them. Help us to seek Your will and Your ways each day. Empower us to be obedient children and faithful soldiers under Your command.

LULLABY HERALDING HIS WATCHFUL CARE

Hallelujah! Sing to the LORD a new song—His praise in the assembly of the godly. Let Israel rejoice[H8055] in their Maker; let the children of Zion rejoice[H1523] in their King. Let them praise His name with dancing, and make music to Him with tambourine and harp. For the LORD takes pleasure in His people; He adorns the afflicted with salvation. Let the saints exult[H5937] in glory; let them shout for joy[H7442] upon their beds.

Psalm 149:1-5

Susan's body may be reclined, but her mind is not confined. She has been "bed-found" since 1997, meaning you will find her in her bed most of the time. From November of 2008 to March of 2011, she was able to get up and out to go to church once a week in a reclining wheelchair. From 2012 to 2016, she could only leave her home on a gurney in an ambulance. Therefore, she only traveled to hospitals unless a friend who owned an ambulance took her to a special event at church. Now Susie and Susan have their own van (PTL!) and are able to go places as long as Susan's pain is somewhat controlled, and two people are available to transfer Susan from the bed to her chair and back again. When we first became roommates, the highlight of our day was the evening ritual we established to sing before we pray and sleep. Susan claims she is brave to sing alongside someone whose bachelor's degree is in Music Education Vocal. However, we lift our hearts to the Lord even if it would be more closely identified as "a joyful noise." We sing songs that praise the Lord for His watchful care over us. The fact that Susan can live pursuing life joyfully and not just want to check out and go home to be with the Lord immediately is proof of the truth in this psalm.

Since the Lord enables Susan to make a joyful noise on her bed, surely, we can all find joy in whatever challenges we are facing. Ask the Lord to show you how to live joyfully through your daily struggles. You might even try singing His praise before you drift off to sleep and again first thing in the morning.

Father, enable us to rise above afflictions to be able to rejoice in all circumstances because we know that You are using every trial to shape us into the image of Your Son, Jesus.

PEACE-FILLED JOY

Deceit is in the hearts of those who devise evil, but the counselors of peace have joy.[H8057]

Proverbs 12:20

In order to be someone who encourages peace, one must intentionally and deliberately emulate the Prince of Peace. If you squeeze a lemon, lemon juice pours from it. If you squeeze a Christian, the Fruit of the Spirit should flow from him or her. Two of the Fruit of the Spirit are peace and joy (Galatians 5:22-23). The Lord encourages those who strive for peace in the Beatitudes when He says, "Blessed are the peacemakers, for they will be called sons of God" (Matthew 5:9).

During my month-long hospital adventure to have both my legs amputated above the knee, I (Susan) knew intense fear and anxiety. Those emotions had to be subdued by the Prince of Peace in order for me to effectively share His gospel. Praise the Lord, He had already given instructions for replacing anxiety with peace:

Philippians 4:6-7 *Be anxious for nothing, but in everything, by prayer and petition, with thanksgiving, present your requests to God. And the peace of God, which surpasses all understanding, will guard your hearts and your minds in Christ Jesus.*

God's grace was paramount during the trial, His peace overshadowing my difficult situation. God brought people of differing faiths to my bedside and enabled me to share His love even in the midst of my pain. I pray that through my testimony, they may find the perfect peace that comes only from trusting the Lord Jesus Christ and discover true joy that is not dependent upon circumstances.

When anxious thoughts begin to well up inside you, immediately bring them to the Lord in prayer, thanking Him in advance for His watchful care for you. He will grant you peace as you trust Him even in the storms of life. He will enable you to have peace-filled joy when you "Cast all your anxiety on Him, because He cares for you" (I Peter 5:7).

Father, we thank You that Your peace enables us to exude joy even during difficult situations. Thank You for holding us securely in Your hand.

Remember that Jesus is with you always, even in the eye of the storm. Perhaps you have experienced His peace when all around you is not peaceful. If so, you can relate to "Eye of the Storm" sung by Ryan Stevenson: https://www.youtube.com/watch?v=X2FqFLKisys

FEASTING ON JOY

A joyful[H8056] heart makes a cheerful[H3190] countenance, but sorrow of the heart crushes the spirit. . .

All the days of the oppressed are bad, but a cheerful[H2896] heart has a continual feast.

Proverbs 15:13 & 15

A joy-filled, cheerful heart never hungers and is always nourished. The Lord blesses those who have an appetite for righteousness and promises their hunger will be satisfied (Matthew 5:6). There are moments of being overwhelmed in this life. When they occur, we need to seek shelter in the Rock of our salvation who renews our joy.

Psalm 61:1-5 *Hear my cry, O God; attend to my prayer. From the ends of the earth I call out to You whenever my heart is faint. Lead me to the rock that is higher than I. For You have been my refuge, a tower of strength against the enemy. Let me dwell in Your tent forever and take refuge in the shelter of Your wings.*

In the journey of my literal pruning, one of the most overwhelming times was when the nurse hit the red button on the wall and called out "Code Blue!" I (Susan) awoke in ICU with a ventilator tube down my throat. Unable to communicate the smallest need or want frustrated me countless times! Even using a "communication board" was nearly impossible because my arm was so weak and tired. Besides that, the letters on the board were not in the best configuration. Spelling each word of a sentence was cumbersome and exacerbating. Susie became pretty good at guessing a word after about three letters which helped a bit. Praise God, I could completely share my aggravations with the Lord because He could translate my thoughts.

Romans 8:26 *In the same way, the Spirit helps us in our weakness. For we do not know how we ought to pray, but the Spirit Himself intercedes for us with groans too deep for words.*

Susie says that even in that situation, I communicated to her the need to share our story of God's love with the hospital staff. I would motion toward the staff member entering the room and then to Susie and myself. She understood this to mean that she was to share the testimony of God's grace, love, and power to use me as a minister and to explain how He had brought the two of us together to be as close as sisters. The joy of the Lord would overcome my frustration and allow me to be His mouthpiece even when I couldn't use my mouth!

Have you partaken of the feast of joy available to you by trusting the Lord Jesus?

Father, we thank You that even when we do not know how to pray, Your Holy Spirit intercedes for us. We thank You that even in the most difficult situations, You help us to experience Your peace and joy!

Remember, you can always run to the Rock. Listen to Whitney Houston singing Dottie Rambo's song, "I Go to the Rock".

https://www.youtube.com/watch?v=yTylq8lhPjc

A WORD FITLY SPOKEN

*A man has joy[H8056] in giving an appropriate answer,
And how good and delightful is a word spoken at the
right moment—how good it is!*
                                    Proverbs 15:23 (AMP)

It is amazing how God uses His sacrifice—plus His story
that comes through One Solitary Life—to touch someone
going through something totally different than you are.
We can tell you that even though we are going through
different trials, we can relate because we know God has
been there through all we are going through. We know
He can bring you through your challenges as well. While
I (Susan) was in the hospital—both before and after the
amputation surgery—I would share a bit of my journey
with the staff. My opening line was, "I can tell what you
do by the color of your scrubs, but you probably can't
guess what I do!" Most of them would have a look that
said, "You do something?" In their defense, I am clas-
sified as quadriplegic and have only limited use of one
arm/hand. I would explain that I am an ordained minister with a master's degree from Oral Roberts University and President of Precious Jewels Ministries, Inc. I
would then encourage them to faithfully follow God's
leading for their lives despite any obstacles or opposi-
tion that seemed to be in the way. Often nurses or care
techs would leave in tears saying that was just what they
needed to hear. God gave me words spoken at the right

moment. What a joy it was to know that God had challenged and blessed people through my witness!

Pray God will give you the encouraging words to uplift someone else when they need it the most. God tells us in Proverbs 25:11 (KJV), "A word fitly spoken is like apples of gold in pictures of silver." Thank Him for the times he has encouraged you through appropriate words fitly spoken by a friend.

Father, may our words always build others up rather than tear them down. May our mouths be used to encourage others and praise You.

THE GREAT PHYSICIAN'S PRESCRIPTION: A DAILY DOSE OF JOY

A joyful heart is good medicine, but a broken spirit dries up the bones.

Proverbs 17:22

Without thinking about the inference, Susie recently complained about her short, stubby legs. Laughing, I replied, "You can't look over at me and say that because I have definitely got you beat in that department. Actually, I think I've cornered the market on that one!" (Both my legs were amputated above the knee.) We both laughed for a long time. Bringing levity into the challenges and trials of life keeps them from defining and depressing me. With the authenticity of God's word and our words, we have the power to define any situation in which we find ourselves. We must learn to see our challenges from a divine perspective, the perspective of God's providence and purpose. It is a day-by-day, sometimes moment-by-moment, struggle to choose to agree with God's direction for our lives. Most of us have our voices and our choices. We can choose life, joy, and godliness daily and can choose to lift our voices in praise to the Lord.

An example of realizing God's divine providence in Scripture is the story of Joseph being sold by his own brothers into slavery because his dreams offended them.

But later he was elevated to a high position in Egypt that ultimately allowed him to save not only his own family but the nation of Israel from annihilation. Joseph became a household servant, then was falsely accused by his owner's wife and cast into prison. The Lord enabled Joseph to interpret dreams for fellow prisoners and eventually to interpret a dream for the Pharaoh. This dream was a prophecy of an upcoming famine. Pharaoh appointed Joseph as his second in command, entrusting him to plan ahead for the preservation of Egypt during the famine. Ironically, the brothers who had sold Joseph into slavery traveled to Egypt to request food for their families. Joseph recognized them, but they did not recognize him because he was now an adult and attired as an Egyptian. When they discovered the true identity of this intimidating authority, they trembled in fear of retaliation, perhaps even fear for their lives. In Genesis 50:20, Joseph said to his brothers, "As for you, what you intended against me for evil, God intended for good, in order to accomplish a day like this—to preserve the lives of many people." Joseph, the dreamer, chose to see the providence of God in his series of painful predicaments and to extend mercy and forgiveness to his brothers.

People laughed at the dream, the vision, the Lord gave to Susan of being His instrument to proclaim His gospel of grace. Many times, she was tempted to believe her purpose would never be fulfilled. She continued to choose joy, finding the humor in her unique predicaments. Today, after writing several books, we continue to trust that Jesus will enable both of us to do all that He calls us to do together.

Allow yourself to seek out humor, particularly in difficult situations. It's okay to laugh. God says it is like medicine. Follow the instructions of the Great Physician and have a joyful heart.

Father, our pursuit of You is intentional and many times intense. However, help us to embrace joy and laughter even during times of trial. You are the Source of our joy.

STAR GAZERS

When they saw the star, they rejoiced[G5463] *with great delight*[G5479].

Matthew 2:10

The magi (wise men) had seen a great star from their country in the east and had read a prophecy of a king to be born of the Jews. They had set out following the star, but it disappeared for a time. They inquired of the Jews' current king, Herod, where this child was to be born. After his scholars informed them the child was to be born in Bethlehem, they set back out on their journey, and the star reappeared. The wise men were not just full of joy when the star came back into view: their joy was exponentially overwhelming. It was also a relief that they could now fulfill their hearts' desire to worship the baby King. They may or may not have understood that the God of the universe was Jesus' Father, but they saw the celestial birthday candle, the ultimate celebratory sign in the heavens, to celebrate the birth of His chosen One. The star, which may have even been the Shekhinah glory of God, led them to the house where Jesus and His earthly parents were staying, and they worshipped Him and gave Him gifts.

Think for just a moment about the glory Jesus left behind in Heaven to endure a humble birth in a stable, being subject to earthly parents, living under the limitations of being a man, and ultimately the sacrifice and humiliation of the cross in order to redeem His forever family. Sometimes the Lord leads us to travel a difficult path. However, we never face a journey as difficult as His incarnation and life among humankind. When you begin to feel that your burdens seem to outweigh your blessings, remember what Jesus suffered for you. Remember that our trials here are but a breath compared to the everlasting glory we will experience because we have surrendered our lives to Jesus. "For our light and momentary affliction is producing for us an eternal weight of glory that is far beyond comparison" 2 Corinthians 4:17. The CNA (Certified Nurse Assistant) who helped Susie care for her mom always told her, "Whatever the Lord calls you to suffer, He will enable you to endure." Even more than that, we know that we will come out victorious! "No, in all these things we are more than conquerors through Him who loved us" (Romans 8:37).

Father, the wise men left their home in the East and traveled a great distance to bring gifts to the Baby King of Israel, Jesus. Lord, help us to follow Your Light wherever You lead us. Help us to constantly seek Your kingdom above all else and trust You to provide our needs (Matthew 6:33). As we seek to follow Your Light, help us to rejoice with great joy like the wise men did so long ago.

Worship with Gaither family of musicians singing "Rejoice with Exceeding Great Joy": https://www.youtube.com/watch?v=cYRrHGE9QJo

Worship with Larry Ford singing "Follow Me": https://www.youtube.com/watch?v=RN8UW_C_sgA

TRUE TREASURE

The kingdom of heaven is like treasure hidden in a field. When a man found it, he hid it again, and in his joy,[G5479] he went and sold all he had and bought that field. Again, the kingdom of heaven is like a merchant in search of fine pearls. When he found one very precious pearl, he went away and sold all he had and bought it.

Matthew 13:44-45

The joy of the kingdom is here and now as well as in eternity. We give up all that we are—our inconsistencies, our incompleteness, our sin—to receive all the purpose and fulfillment that Jesus is and wants to reveal through our lives. We also give up any claim to our achievements and endeavors. Paul says that everything "good" about him was waste material compared to the righteousness of Jesus and all that the Lord has to offer:

Philippians 3:7-9 (VOICE) B*ut whatever I used to count as my greatest accomplishments, I've written off as a loss because of the Anointed One. And more so, I now realize that all I gained and thought was important was nothing but yesterday's garbage compared to knowing the Anointed Jesus as my Lord. For Him I have thrown everything aside—it's nothing but a pile of waste—so that I may gain Him. When it counts, I want to be found belonging to Him, not clinging to my own righteousness based on law, but actively relying on the faithfulness of the Anointed One. This is true righteousness, supplied by God, acquired by faith.*

Susan's legs were literally "a pile of waste." The doctor described them as "ticking time bombs" because necrotic ulcers—dying flesh—covered both legs from just below the knee to the bottoms of her feet. Amputation seemed to be the only solution. You may think that giving up her legs in order to live longer to serve the Lord was easy since she had never really walked. However, when her teenaged niece and goddaughter first suggested the idea of cutting off the bad legs in order to have more of a life, Susan was appalled. Give up a part of herself? The majority of society had never seen her as whole. How much would that intensify when she was missing approximately one-third of her height, both legs? When she was eight years old, a stranger asked her Nana, "Why would you bring that out in public? Why should we have to look at that?!" What cruel comments would she hear when her legs were gone? However, knowing that the Lord would have her choose life, and reflecting on what her niece had suggested out of a pure love for her and not desiring to see her in pain, she eventually made the difficult decision to have both legs amputated above the knee. God had used Rylee to plant the seed of removing the legs which ultimately gave me the courage to suggest amputation to my doctors. Looking back, we now know the Lord used the time in the hospital to minister to people, to grow us closer to Him, and to strengthen the bond between us (Susan and Susie), to do His work. For every inch of height lost, we believe we have gained exponentially spiritually!

The true treasure is Jesus Himself! Knowing Him is worth more than any earthly accumulation or even our "rights" to our own bodies. Rather than succumb to the toxicity of her legs and go home to Heaven, Susan surrendered one-third of her height in order to live out God's purpose for her here which brings her true joy. Is there anything you are valuing more than your relationship with the Lord Jesus and your God-given purpose? Give up even the greatest wealth you have to gain the only true treasure, a relationship with the Lord Jesus Christ who is the Source of true joy!

Father, help us to value You above all else. Help us to prioritize studying Your word, to know You more completely. Help us to surrender anything that stands in the way of serving You and building Your kingdom!

JOYFUL TREMBLING

But the angel said to the women, "Do not be afraid, for I know that you are looking for Jesus, who was crucified. He is not here; He has risen, just as He said! Come, see the place where He lay. Then go quickly and tell His disciples, 'He has risen from the dead and is going ahead of you into Galilee. There you will see Him.' See, I have told you." So they hurried away from the tomb in fear and great joy[G5479], and ran to tell His disciples.

Matthew 28:5-8

Fear and joy going on at the same time seems contradictory. To have the two emotions simultaneously may seem impossible. However, remembering that the women who had gone to Jesus's tomb to anoint His body and prepare Him for burial had just had an encounter with a celestial being rightly accounts for the fear, and the joy was their reaction to the angel's message that Jesus was risen from the dead. They were filled with exuberance at the reality of Jesus's resurrection and at the fact that they were given the privilege to announce this miracle to their brethren, the disciples. They were also filled with joy that they were soon to see Jesus in Galilee as the angel had said. Then they were surprised at Jesus standing before them! He repeated the instruction the angel had given them to tell the disciples to meet Him in Galilee.

I (Susan) know from experience that fear and joy can be present simultaneously. Parked in front of the lights and cameras, I experienced stage fright. This was my first time on national television. I was being interviewed by James Robison on his program "Life Today." The first few minutes of speaking in public always feel awkward to me because I do not know the people in the audience, and they do not know me. About three minutes into this interview, I was calm; and speech was flowing due to the presence of the Lord. After a few more moments, I noticed studio personnel being moved to the point of tears. The Lord replaced my trepidation with overflowing joy in the presence of His Holy Spirit.

The women at the tomb knew the panic of being startled by an angel coinciding with the joy of realizing Jesus was alive! Let us not be calloused to the wonderment of the empty tomb just because we have heard the story every Resurrection Sunday since we were children. Let us never lose the awe we experienced the first time were heard about Jesus rising from the dead. Does the power of God demonstrated in the resurrection of our Lord fill you with joyful amazement?

Father, may we never forget the wonder of the death, burial, and resurrection of our Lord Jesus Christ. Fill us with trembling joy as we meditate on Your awesome power!

ANSWERED PRAYER RESULTS IN REJOICING

But the angel said to him, "Do not be afraid, Zechariah, because your prayer has been heard. Your wife Elizabeth will bear you a son, and you are to give him the name John. He will be a joy^{G5479} *and delight*^{G20} *to you, and many will rejoice*^{G5463} *at his birth, for he will be great in the sight of the Lord. He shall never take wine or strong drink, and he will be filled with the Holy Spirit even from his mother's womb.*

Luke 1:13-15

This was a huge moment in Zechariah's life even before the angel startled him. It was truly a "once in a lifetime opportunity" in his service to the Lord as a priest:

> Each of the twenty-four divisions served in the temple for one week, twice a year, as well as at the major festivals. An individual priest, however, could offer the incense at the daily sacrifice only once in his lifetime since there were so many priests. Therefore this was the climactic moment of Zechariah's priestly career, perhaps the most dramatic moment possible for the event described to have occurred. God was breaking into the ancient routine of Jewish ritual with the word of his decisive saving act. (41)

Zechariah would have been offering incense on behalf of all the people of Israel. Incense burned before the Lord was a symbol of prayer. The angel said the Lord had heard Zechariah's prayer. What prayers would Zechariah bring before the Lord?

> 13 This is the first indication of prayer on the part of Zechariah. The specific petition probably refers to both his lifelong prayer for a child (probably a son) and his just-offered prayer in the temple for the messianic redemption of Israel. (42)

At that moment in the Holy Place, Zechariah would have been praying for the Messiah to come to redeem Israel. However, he and Elizabeth had probably prayed often for a child, particularly a son to carry on his name. Both prayers were being answered in the birth of John. He would not only be a joy and delight to his parents, but the entire community would rejoice because a barren woman had been given a son!

The angel foretold that John would be filled with the Holy Spirit while still in Elizabeth's womb! He would be set apart as a special servant of God from the start. In fact, he first recognized Jesus as the Messiah while they were both still in utero! Susan says, "John was the first holy roller as he jumped for joy inside his mother's body at the sound of Mary's voice!" When he was an adult, as forerunner of the Messiah, John would prepare the

Jews for great rejoicing. He would be the prophet that first identified Jesus as the Messiah, the "Lamb of God".

John 1:29 *The next day John saw Jesus coming toward him and said, "Look, the Lamb of God, who takes away the sin of the world!*

Do we recognize the tremendous gift God has given us in the form of His Son born as a human baby? Do we rejoice at the sound of His name? Does the "Good News" of God's grace in sending Jesus to die in our place, still make us want to shout praises? Heart check: do you need to rejoice (return to your joy) today?

Father, help us to rejoice, to remember the Source of our joy daily.

When Elizabeth heard Mary's greeting, the baby leaped in her womb, and Elizabeth was filled with the Holy Spirit. In a loud voice she exclaimed, "Blessed are you among women, and blessed is the fruit of your womb! And why am I so honored, that the mother of my Lord should come to me? For as soon as the sound of your greeting reached my ears, the baby in my womb leaped for joy[G20]. Blessed is she who has believed that the Lord's word to her will be fulfilled."

Luke 1:41-45

Children are indeed a heritage from the LORD, and the fruit of the womb is His reward.

Psalm 127:3

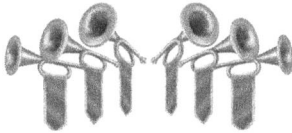

JOHN JUMPS FOR JOY

Unborn baby in the womb,
at Mary's greeting, John jumped for joy.
Filled with the Spirit from conception,
he knew Messiah's mother's voice.
The Holy Spirit filled Elizabeth's heart
and enabled her to know
the presence of her Lord and Savior
in a holy Embryo.

Yet today's society justifies
the murder of an unborn baby,
debating when embryo becomes a person,
with no thought that maybe
since children are a gift from God
and the fruit of the womb a reward,
A fertilized egg, an embryo,
is declared a human soul by the Lord.
If you have already had an abortion,
you will find no judgment here.
Mary's baby was born to redeem you.
Forgiveness is yours! Draw near
to Jesus who bore our sins on the cross,
the Lamb of God, our sacrifice.
Raised to life, He conquered the grave
and offers you paradise!

UNBORN BABY'S PRAISE

For as soon as the sound of your greeting reached my ears, the baby in my womb leaped for joy.[G20]

Luke 1:44

The exclamation in the Scripture above was made by Elizabeth when her relative, Mary, came to visit her. Elizabeth was pregnant with the baby who would eventually become known as John the Baptist. The Holy Spirit revealed to fetus John that Mary was carrying the Messiah. Unborn John, utterly ecstatic, did gymnastics in his mother's womb. Elizabeth, also moved by the Holy Spirit, interpreted her baby's moves as leaping for joy. An UNBORN baby was the first to recognize our Savior, who was yet an EMBRYO. This is a strong argument for the fact that a fetus or even an embryo is already a person God has formed inside the mother-to-be. We are designed with purpose and intention from the beginning. In Psalm 139:13 (VOICE), the psalmist states, "For You shaped me, inside and out. You knitted me together in my mother's womb long before I took my first breath." Apparently, knitting is not just for "little old ladies." The Lord is a master knitter because He knit each of us together within our mother's wombs. That's a lot of knitting! God creates and knows intimately each embryo while still in the womb. God told Jeremiah, "Before I even formed you in your mother's womb, I knew all about you. Before you drew your first breath, I had already chosen you to be My prophet to speak My word to the nations" Jeremiah 1:4–5 (VOICE).

Before I was born, God created me for His purpose, to be His mouthpiece for His glory. He also knew I would face the daunting limitations of cerebral palsy. There are people who would have given up on a child with so many complexities. However, God placed many people in my life over the years to encourage me to be an overcomer rather than to wallow in self-pity. Knowing I would need a facilitator to accomplish my God-given purpose, the Lord formed Susie and used godly people to shape her into the person she is today. There are those who would end the life of an embryo, fetus, or even a baby thought to be less than "normal" before that child ever had an opportunity to live. Praise the Lord, He did not allow this to happen to me! God creates each one of us in the womb. That embryo, fetus, or baby is a person from the moment of conception, and to destroy that life is mur-der. One thing we must remember is that Jesus died to provide forgiveness for those who have made the choice to have an abortion. If you have had an abortion and you belong to Jesus, do not let Satan keep throwing that back at you. Memorize Romans 8:1, "Therefore, there is now no condemnation for those who are in Christ Je-sus." You are forgiven. You are loved. You can be an in-strument of God's grace to bless others. You are God's precious jewel, and He wants you to fill you with the joy Christ died to provide for you!

An unborn fetus expressed exuberant joy due to the upcoming arrival of our Savior. How much more should we, who know the rest of the story, rejoice?

Father, we thank You for the gift of being born and even more so, for the gift of being born again by Your grace. We thank You that You designed us for a purpose and will enable us to fulfill that purpose in Your strength and for Your glory.

MARY MAGNIFIES THE LORD REJOICING IN SONG

Then Mary said: "My soul magnifies the Lord, and my spirit rejoices^{G2}1 in God my Savior! For He has looked with favor on the humble state of His servant. From now on all generations will call me blessed.

Luke 1:46-48

Baby John was not the only one who was jumping for joy (Luke 1:44). Mary, under the influence of the Holy Spirit, burst into a poetic song sometimes referred to as The Magnificat. Every fiber of Mary's being declared the greatness of her God who had transformed her into the mother of her own Savior. One of no special significance was carrying the One of supreme significance. John the Baptist would later declare, "He must increase, but I must decrease," (John 3:30); and Mary understood this concept well. She sang, not to draw attention to herself but to lift high the praises of God. She realized that God had chosen her, a humble but devout Jewish girl from a town known for no-goods. God chose a lowly peasant girl—probably a teenager—to be the mother of His only begotten Son because He was sending His Son to serve rather than to be served.

Matthew 20:26b-28 . . . *whoever wants to become great among you must be your servant, and whoever wants to be first among you must be your slave— just as the Son of Man did not come to be served, but to serve, and to give His life as a ransom for many."*

All generations have recognized the blessing God bestowed upon Mary, but those who read the gospels know that she endured much sorrow along with experiencing great joy. Mary is a prime example of how God chooses those who men would not necessarily choose. He chooses the weak to confound the mighty (1 Corinthians 1:27). Do not say to yourself that our omnipotent God cannot use you in mighty ways because you are weak, not very bright, too bad, or whatever excuse you come up with. None of us can have any worthwhile effect until we are in His hands, but the humblest life when fully committed and submitted to the Lord will be used to help turn the world upside down!

Acts 17:5b-6 *They raided Jason's house in search of Paul and Silas, hoping to bring them out to the people. But when they could not find them, they dragged Jason and some other brothers before the city officials, shouting, "These men who have turned the world upside down have now come here."*

Father, like Mary, we are amazed that You have chosen us, not only to be adopted into Your family but to have the privilege of speaking and teaching the truths found in Your word. Thank You for Your amazing grace!

Enjoy Mark Lowry, Guy Penrod, and David Phelps singing "Mary, Did You Know?": https://www.youtube.com/watch?v=3fbgWa5pH3g

with no blemish or spot be sacrificed to Him to atone for the people's sins. John the Baptist declared, "Look, the Lamb of God, who takes away the sin of the world! (John 1:29b). Jesus, the final perfect sinless Passover Lamb, chose to die on the cross in our place to pay for our sins. He rose again to bring all those who trust and believe in Him into the perfect kingdom of love, peace, and joy.

I (Susan) realized the truth that Jesus died for me at a very early age. I was about four or five years old, sitting in church with my granddad. Even before the pastor invited all those who wanted to surrender their lives to Jesus to come to the altar, I told my granddad that I wanted to go. I didn't want to be separated from Jesus. I wanted to be on His team and live with Him forever someday in heaven. So, my granddad took me up in his arms and carried me, heavy metal and leather leg braces and all, to the altar. I told the preacher, Brother T.D. Hall, "I want to receive Jesus into my heart. I want to live with Him, be on His team, and not be His enemy." From that day forward, the Holy Spirit has lived in me. I am a citizen of His kingdom even while I am still in this earth-suit. Someday, I will live with Him in the forever home He has prepared for all those who love Him. If you have trusted Jesus as your Savior, He has brought you into His kingdom, too. Rejoice!!!

Philippians 3:20-21 *But our citizenship is in heaven, and we eagerly await a Savior from there, the Lord Jesus Christ, who, by the power that enables Him to subject all things to Himself, will transform our lowly bodies to be like His glorious body.*

Father, thank You for sending Jesus to redeem us and set us free from the slavery of sin. Thank You for His promise to prepare a place for us and return to take us into His home.

"Celebrate the Child" with Michael Card: https://www.youtube.com/watch?v=jXGiYOIJtec

And listen to "Scandalon" also by Michael Card: https://www.youtube.com/watch?v=6Vj6Rv5WvIo

REJOICE! THE REDEEMER IS FINALLY HERE

But the angel said to them, "Do not be afraid! For behold, I bring you good news of great joy^{G5479} that will be for all the people: Today in the city of David a Savior has been born to you. He is Christ the Lord! And this will be a sign to you: You will find a baby wrapped in swaddling cloths and lying in a manger."

Luke 2:10-12

The great joy the angels proclaimed was not to be for the Jews only but for all nations, all those who come to know Jesus. Repeatedly, the news of Jesus' birth is declared to be a joyous occasion. The long-awaited Messiah—the Redeemer— had arrived and would eventually offer Himself up as a sacrifice to rescue those who trust in Him from suffering the wrath of God and the penalty of their sins. Israel, a nation conquered by Rome, had been plunged into deep darkness and many erroneously thought the Messiah would free them from the tyranny of Rome. Jesus was not the military conqueror whom they were expecting and for whom they hoped. However, He freed them from the greater captivity of sin, bringing those who believe and trust in Him an overwhelming peace and everlasting joy. They were looking for Jesus to be a conqueror and set up a powerful kingdom, to lead them into battle, and to overthrow Rome. However, He came as a Lamb led silently to slaughter (Isaiah 53:7). The Law God gave to Moses required that lambs with no blemish or spot be sacrificed to Him to atone for the people's sins. John the Baptist declared, "Look, the Lamb of God, who takes away the sin of the world! (John 1:29b). Jesus, the final perfect sinless Passover Lamb, chose to die on the cross in our place to pay for our sins. He rose again to bring all those who trust and believe in Him into the perfect kingdom of love, peace, and joy.

I (Susan) realized the truth that Jesus died for me at a very early age. I was about four or five years old, sitting in church with my granddad. Even before the pastor invited all those who wanted to surrender their lives to Jesus to come to the altar, I told my granddad that I wanted to go. I didn't want to be separated from Jesus. I wanted to be on His team and live with Him forever someday in heaven. So, my granddad took me up in his arms and carried me, heavy metal and leather leg braces and all, to the altar. I told the preacher, Brother T.D. Hall, "I want to receive Jesus into my heart. I want to live with Him, be on His team, and not be His enemy." From that day forward, the Holy Spirit has lived in me. I am a citizen of His kingdom even while I am still in this earth-suit. Someday, I will live with Him in the forever home He has prepared for all those who love Him. If you have trusted Jesus as your Savior, He has brought you into His kingdom, too. Rejoice!!!

Philippians 3:20-21 *But our citizenship is in heaven, and we eagerly await a Savior from there, the Lord Jesus Christ, who, by the power that enables Him to subject all things to Himself, will transform our lowly bodies to be like His glorious body.*

Father, thank You for sending Jesus to redeem us and set us free from the slavery of sin. Thank You for His promise to prepare a place for us and return to take us into His home.

"Celebrate the Child" with Michael Card: https://www.youtube.com/watch?v=jXGiYOIJtec

And listen to "Scandalon" also by Michael Card: https://www.youtube.com/watch?v=6Vj6Rv5WvIo

AN OVERCOMER'S JOY

Blessed are you when people hate you, and when they exclude you and insult you and reject your name as evil because of the Son of Man. Rejoice[G5463] in that day and leap for joy[G4640], because great is your reward in heaven. For their fathers treated the prophets in the same way.

Luke 6:22-23

During my senior year at Bob Hope High School, I (Susan) could have had a full ride scholarship to any college in Texas, but I had a firm conviction from the Lord that I was to attend Oral Roberts University in Oklahoma. A few students and faculty members did not know quite how to take this news. Some students would laugh and make fun of ORU's founder, Oral Roberts. However, I had to go where God had called me. I would not be discouraged or dissuaded by their negative responses. I was trying to secure scholarships and grants. Therefore, I wrote letters seeking more financial assistance. Knowing that I had some physical disabilities, they were not quick to send back information. There are limitations in most people's lives. In my eyes, these are only challenges to be overcome. The administrators at that time at ORU were concerned about how I could facilitate living in a dorm and getting to class each day successfully. With the help of my grandparents and my cousin Natalie, I put flyers all over campus advertising for personal attendants because I was not allowed to register until I had secured attendant care.

God was then, is now, and ever will be faithful. The Lord provided students I trained to meet my personal needs—assistance with eating, grooming, transfers, etc. The university provided students to transcribe my dictated papers and assist me with taking notes on my reading assignments. I lived successfully in the dorm for eight years while earning two degrees. The fact that I made it through college is evidence of God's will prevailing against all odds. At the end of my undergraduate studies, I received the first ever "Overcomer's Award" which was given to the student at ORU who excelled under seemingly unsurmountable challenges. In addition to the inherent difficulties of attending classes in a power chair, I had suffered from walking pneumonia the last semester of my undergraduate studies!

When naysayers try to discourage us, we must rejoice in knowing that our God will enable us to fulfill the calling He has given us. John 6:33 says, "I have told you these things so that in Me you may have peace. In the world you will have tribulation. But take courage; I have overcome the world!" You, too, can be an overcomer as you trust Jesus to be your enablement in all you do. You will be able to rejoice in the trials as you trust in the One who has overcome them and will bring you through them successfully as well.

Father, help our joy to never wane even in the most difficult struggles or persecutions. Help us to remain secure in Your love and Your ability to see us through each trial.

Worship with Mandisa singing "Overcomer":
https://www.youtube.com/watch?v=z29olPjFbqg

IS YOUR NAME WRITTEN IN THE LAMB'S BOOK OF LIFE?

The seventy-two returned with joy[G5479] *and said, "Lord, even the demons submit to us in Your name." So He told them, "I saw Satan fall like lightning from heaven. Behold, I have given you authority to tread on snakes and scorpions, and over all the power of the enemy. Nothing will harm you. Nevertheless, do not rejoice*[G5463] *that the spirits submit to you, but rejoice*[G5463] *that your names are written in heaven."*

Luke 10:17-20

Jesus had sent seventy of His followers in pairs to preach and minister in His name. They returned recounting the tremendous experiences they had on the journey. They were amazed that He had given them authority to cast out demons, but Jesus made it clear that they were rejoicing in the wrong things. What they should rejoice in was not the power to cast out demons or do other miracles; it was the fact that their names were on the roll call for Heaven. Our greatest joy should be the certainty of our salvation and that we are adopted into God's forever family. If the Lord were to heal me (Susan) completely tomorrow—Yes, I believe that He still works miracles of healing today and am trusting Him to perform one!—of course I would leap for joy. However, I can already rejoice in the fact that I will be totally restored physically, emotionally, and spiritually in that day when I join Him, either by death or meeting

Him in the air when He returns for His church. God already sees me as I will be!

Is your name written in the Lamb's Book of Life? Have you surrendered yourself completely to the Lord Jesus? If you are uncertain about any part of becoming a follower of Jesus, please read the "Jewels of Salvation" and "Believers' Benefits" in the back of this book. From the moment you accept Jesus's invitation until the moment He receives you home, your joy will progressively increase as the Holy Spirit makes you more and more like Jesus.

Romans 8:29 *For those God foreknew, He also predestined to be conformed to the image of His Son, so that He would be the firstborn among many brothers.*

Father, we rejoice that Your grace has set us free from the power of sin and Satan. Our greatest joy is the assurance that our names are written in the Lamb's Book of Life meaning that we will spend eternity with Jesus in perfect joy and peace.

WHAT GAVE JESUS ECSTATIC JOY?

At that time Jesus rejoiced[G21] in the Holy Spirit and declared, "I praise You, Father, Lord of heaven and earth, because You have hidden these things from the wise and learned, and revealed them to little children. Yes, Father, for this was well-pleasing in Your sight."

Luke 10:21

At that moment he was filled with joy[G21] by the Ruach HaKodesh and said, "Father, Lord of heaven and earth, I thank you because you concealed these things from the sophisticated and educated, yet revealed them to ordinary people. Yes, Father, I thank you that it pleased you to do this.

Luke 10:21 (CJB)

At that same time Jesus was filled with the joy[G21] of the Holy Spirit, and he said, "O Father, Lord of heaven and earth, thank you for hiding these things from those who think themselves wise and clever, and for revealing them to the childlike. Yes, Father, it pleased you to do it this way.

Luke 10:21 (NLT)

G21 agalliáō; contracted agalliō̄, fut. agalliásō, aor. ēgallíasa, from ágan (n.f.), much, and hállomai (242), to leap. To exult, leap for joy, to show one's joy by leaping and skipping denoting excessive or ecstatic joy and delight. Hence in the NT to rejoice, exult. Often spoken of rejoicing with song and dance (Sept.: Ps. 2:11; 20:5; 40:16; 68:3). Usually found in the mid. deponent agalliáomai. (I) Used in an absolute sense (Acts 2:26, "my tongue was glad," meaning I rejoiced in words, sang aloud; Luke 10:21; Acts 16:34). (43)

10:21 Infants here refers to those who trusted in Jesus's words and works through childlike faith. (44)

What made Jesus ecstatic? He was rejoicing because common men were able to come into the kingdom of God in childlike faith. The religious and intellectual elite—Scribes, Pharisees, and Sadducees—who should have recognized Him as fulfilling all the prophecies concerning the Messiah, were too busy making a show of their piety to see the simple truth before them. Jesus praised the Father for choosing to make salvation accessible to common, everyday people. In fact, elsewhere Jesus proclaimed that childlikeness is a must:

Luke 18:16-17 *But Jesus called the children to Him and said, "Let the little children come to Me, and do not hinder them! For the kingdom of God belongs to such as these. Truly I tell you, anyone who does not receive the kingdom of God like a little child will never enter it."*

What kind of faith does a child have? Children, unless they have been abused or neglected, are extremely trusting. They stand on the edge of the pool and shout, "catch me," believing mom or dad will be right there! They have no fear that their loving parent will let them fall. Do we have that simple, childlike trust in Jesus? We need not, and cannot, do anything to redeem ourselves from sin or earn our way into heaven. Our total trust must be in Jesus who paid the penalty for our sin and conquered death and the grave. All we need to do is accept the gift He purchased for us which is eternal life.

Father, we rejoice that we do not have to be intellectual giants to understand the Gospel. We thank You for making it simple enough for Susan to give her life to Jesus before the age of five and Susie to surrender her life to Him at the age of fifteen. Please keep us from over-complicating Your word!

In the same way, I tell you, there is joy[5479] in the pres-
ence of God's angels over one sinner who repents.

Luke 15:10

WHAT MAKES GOD
AND HIS ANGELS REJOICE?

The shepherd rejoiced when he found his lost sheep
and immediately gathered all of his peeps
to celebrate with him the lamb's return.

The woman rejoiced when she found her lost coin
and called all her friends so they could join
her rejoicing over finding the money she'd earned.

The father rejoiced when his son came back home,
forgave him for recklessly choosing to roam,
killed the fatted calf for a big barbecue.

All this rejoicing is minor compared
to the party in Heaven the angels share
with God for one sinner who Jesus makes new.

JESUS SEEKS ALL KINDS OF PEOPLE

Then Jesus entered Jericho and was passing through. And there was a man named Zacchaeus, a chief tax collector, who was very wealthy. He was trying to see who Jesus was, but could not see over the crowd because he was small in stature. So he ran on ahead and climbed a sycamore tree to see Him, since Jesus was about to pass that way. When Jesus came to that place, He looked up and said, "Zacchaeus, hurry down, for I must stay at your house today." So Zacchaeus hurried down and welcomed Him joyfully.[G5463] And all who saw this began to grumble, saying, "He has gone to be the guest of a sinful man!" But Zacchaeus stood up and said to the Lord, "Look, Lord, half of my possessions I give to the poor, and if I have cheated anyone, I will repay it fourfold." Jesus said to him, "Today salvation has come to this house, because this man too is a son of Abraham. For the Son of Man came to seek and to save the lost."

Luke 19:1-10

Zacchaeus's stature or lack thereof did not keep him from seeing Jesus. For some strange reason, Susan can relate to him. Really not strange at all because in 2015, she gave up twenty-three inches of her physical height. Following her leg amputations, she is now thirty-eight inches tall! Though Zacchaeus was small, he had to be strong and agile to run ahead and climb up a tree to have a better view. Jesus foreknew Zacchaeus's situation and knew that he would be in the tree. He looked up and invited Himself to dinner at the tax collector's house in order to bring him salvation. The saving grace of God trumped the social grace of waiting for an invitation to eat and stay at someone's home. Jesus does not wait for us to invite Him in. He invites us and the Holy Spirit actively pursues us until we respond. Zacchaeus exuberantly climbed down the tree and received Christ with exceeding joy. From this encounter, Zacchaeus's life was forever transformed, which is evidenced by the fact that he gave half of his goods to the poor and restored four-fold to all those from whom he previously had fraudulently swindled. In so doing, Zachaeus was doing even more than the restitution specified in the Mosaic Law:

19:8 I restore fourfold. Zacchaeus' willingness to make restitution was proof that his conversion was genuine. It was the fruit, not the condition, of his salvation. The law required a penalty of one-fifth as restitution for money acquired by fraud (Lev. 6:5; Num. 5:6, 7), so Zacchaeus was doing more than was required. The law required 4-fold restitution only when an animal was stolen and killed (Ex. 22:1). If the animal was found alive, only two-fold restitution was required (Ex. 22:4). But Zacchaeus judged his own crime severely, acknowledging that he was as guilty as the lowest common robber. Since much of his wealth had probably been acquired fraudulently, this was a costly commitment. On top of that, he gave half his goods to the poor. But Zacchaeus had just found incomprehensible spiritual riches and did not mind the loss of material wealth (see notes on 14:28; Matt. 13:44–46).(45)

The grumblers complained that Jesus was eating at the house of a sinner, but Jesus had come to seek out the lost people. People like little Zacchaeus. People like you and me. All kinds of people—short, tall, fat, thin, brilliant, not so bright. What we all have in common is that we have sinned. Jesus offers us freedom from the slavery of sin.

Romans 3:23-24 (NLT) *For everyone has sinned; we all fall short of God's glorious standard. Yet God, in his grace, freely makes us right in his sight. He did this through Christ Jesus when he freed us from the penalty for our sins.*

If the Holy Spirit has tugged at your heart to draw you into a relationship with Jesus, have you answered "yes" joyfully? Are you and others seeing evidence of the change He is making in your life? Are you beginning to see the Fruit of the Spirit growing in you?

Father, thank You for sending Your Son, Jesus, to live among us and proclaim Your love, to die in our place on the cross, and to be raised from the dead as a demon-

stration of Your power to resurrect us! Thank you for drawing us to You that we might partake of Your grace and experience exuberant joy!

TOO GOOD TO BE TRUE?

Now their fear gives way to joy^G5479; but it seems too good to be true, and they're still unsure.

Luke 24:41a

The disciples in Jerusalem had been joined by two disciples who had talked with Jesus on their way home to Emmaus. Those in Jerusalem testified that Jesus was alive and appeared to Simon Peter, and the Emmaus travelers told how He had explained Scripture to them and revealed Himself as He broke bread and blessed it. Suddenly Jesus appears in the middle of them even though they were in a room with the door locked! At first, they were terrified, thinking He was a ghost. Then Jesus invited them to examine Him closely and even touch Him to prove He had flesh and bones. Now their abject terror turned to joyful confetti bursting forth inside them, and they were exuberant. However, the whole situation made their brains go tilt. A little nagging voice in their heads tells them it is all too awesome to be real, too good to be true. Jesus patiently indulged their doubt and proved the reality of His bodily resurrection by eating a piece of fish in their presence.

When presenting the Gospel, we are sometimes met with skepticism. Salvation, forgiveness, and Heaven without having to do anything to earn them seems too good to be true. However, the fact is that we could never be good enough to earn or deserve what God has offered us for free. Jesus died to make our salvation possible. It was not free to Jesus because He paid the price for us. Scripture confirms that salvation is a free gift. The facts are there. We can only present them and pray the Holy Spirit opens the eyes of the person in need of Jesus.

Father, like these first disciples, You sometimes inundate us with undeniable facts, yet we still doubt. Father, please forgive us for doubting and increase our faith!

ANTICIPATORY JOY

"And behold, I am sending the promise of My Father upon you. But remain in the city until you have been clothed with power from on high." When Jesus had led them out as far as Bethany, He lifted up His hands and blessed them. While He was blessing them, He left them and was carried up into heaven. And they worshiped Him and returned to Jerusalem with great joy,[G5479] praising God continually in the temple.

Luke 24:49-53

It would have to have been a miraculous occurrence that the disciples could rejoice even though their Rabbi, their Savior, was leaving them. Before Jesus was caught up in the clouds, He had given them confidence that the promised Comforter, the Holy Spirit, would come to them in Jerusalem. They were instructed to wait in the city for this promise to be fulfilled. The presence of the Holy Spirit would strengthen and maintain the intimacy that each one of the disciples, including the women who had followed Him, had enjoyed with Jesus in their everyday, present, tangible experiences with Him. When the Spirit came upon them, it was in the form of a rushing, mighty wind and tongues of flame! They were immediately enabled to testify about Jesus boldly in languages they had never studied!

Acts 2:1-6 *When the day of Pentecost came, they were all together in one place. Suddenly a sound like a mighty rushing wind came from heaven and filled the whole house where they were sitting. They saw tongues like flames of fire that separated and came to rest on each of them. And they were all filled with the Holy Spirit and began to speak in other tongues as the Spirit enabled them. Now there were dwelling in Jerusalem God-fearing Jews from every nation under heaven. And when this sound rang out, a crowd came together in bewilderment, because each one heard them speaking his own language.*

Even though we no longer perceive God in the person of Jesus with our five senses, His presence is still strong in the lives of believers via the work of the Holy Spirit. The way we now maintain an intimate relationship with our Lord is by Bible study, illuminated by the Spirit within us, and by prayer. How much time do you devote to developing this most important of all relationships? Are you reading the word with anticipatory joy, looking forward in eager expectation to how the Holy Spirit will move in your life?

Father, we can have joy now while we look forward to what You will do in and through us in the future. Let us wait joyfully, praising You continually, like the disciples waited in Jerusalem for the promised Holy Spirit.

ABIDING JOY

If you keep My commandments, you will remain in My love, just as I have kept My Father's commandments and remain in His love. I have told you these things so that My joy^{G5479} may be in you and your joy^{G5479} may be complete. This is My commandment, that you love one another as I have loved you.

John 15:10-12

Joy is conditional upon the act of abiding in our loving relationship with God the Father and Jesus the Son through the indwelling of the Holy Spirit. Father, Son, and Holy Spirit are perfected in their love. We do not love perfectly. We are messes being made into messages of God's love, goodness, and grace. As we grow in our ability to love the Lord and people, our joy will increase. Part of this is not being "in love" with ourselves but loving ourselves. Matthew 22:37-39 (ESV) "And he said to him, 'You shall love the Lord your God with all your heart and with all your soul and with all your mind. This is the great and first commandment. And a second is like it: You shall love your neighbor as yourself.'" It is important to note that we cannot give away what we do not have. If we haven't experienced and understood the love of God, we cannot properly love ourselves or others. Have you personally experienced God's love in your life? If so, are you sharing it with others? If not, I pray the Lord will send someone to share His love with you. When we are confident in God's love for us, we experience true joy.

Father, may we increasingly experience the joy of loving unconditionally as You do. As we abide in Your love and share that love with others, please cause joy to abide in us as well—joy that cannot be shaken by circumstances because we are secure in Your love.

IRREVOCABLE JOY

So also you have sorrow now, but I will see you again and your hearts will rejoice[G5463], and no one will take away your joy[G5479]. In that day you will no longer ask Me anything. Truly, truly, I tell you, whatever you ask the Father in My name, He will give you. Until now you have not asked for anything in My name. Ask and you will receive, so that your joy[G5479] may be complete.

John 16:22-24

Jesus had just explained that He was going to die, and the disciples would temporarily be without him. After His resurrection, their sorrow would be turned to joy. This joy that would come to them would be a forever, complete joy. It could not be snatched away by any earthly circumstance. Salvation, healing, and deliverance are found in the name of Jesus. In order to use "in Jesus's name", one must have a personal relationship with Jesus; and one must also know, according to the Scriptures, what Jesus teaches us concerning His will. Requesting something in the power of Jesus's name implies that one is submitting to the will of God. When we ask in the power of His name, in the will of the Lord, we will experience true, total joy.

Before you petition God, do you make sure that your petition meets with His will as revealed in the Bible? If so, you can pray expecting an answer. His answer may not always be exactly what you were thinking of, but it will be exactly what you need and will ultimately bring glory to God as well as joy to you. The joy that Jesus gives us is everlasting. He will never go back on His promises. We can remain joyfully confident in that truth.

Father, help us to discern Your will according to Your word, the Bible. Strengthen us—physically, spiritually, emotionally, and mentally—to fulfill the calling You have given us. Thank You for Your forgiveness and grace when we fail.

JOY FULFILLED

Holy Father, protect them by Your name, the name You gave Me, so that they may be one as We are one. While I was with them, I protected and preserved them by Your name, the name You gave Me. Not one of them has been lost, except the son of destruction, so that the Scripture would be fulfilled. But now I am coming to You; and I am saying these things while I am in the world, so that they may have My joy[G5479] *fulfilled within them. I have given them Your word and the world has hated them; for they are not of the world, just as I am not of the world.*

John 17:11-14

God's word and the world system are contrasted as polar opposites. When we study Scripture, we should go one step further to meditate on it, to internalize it. In other words, the truth of the Word is walked out in our everyday lives through our thinking, speaking, and interacting with family, co-workers, and strangers. The Bible brings joy because it is living; it is as relevant today as when it was first written. We can have joy because in the Word we find peace to replace anxiety: "Be anxious for nothing, but in everything, by prayer and petition, with thanksgiving, present your requests to God. And the peace of God, which surpasses all understanding, will guard your hearts and your minds in Christ Jesus" (Philippians 4:6-7), power and love to replace fear: "For God has not given us a spirit of fear, but of power, love, and self-control" (2 Timothy 1:7), and direction to replace aimlessness: "Trust in the LORD with all your heart, and lean not on your own understanding; in all your ways acknowledge Him, and He will make your paths straight" (Proverbs 3:5-6). The Bible is a treasure trove of joy for those who believe. "Your words became to me a joy and the delight of my heart" (Jer. 15:16). "I rejoice in the way of Your testimonies as much as in all riches." (Ps. 119:14). "I rejoice in Your promise like one who finds great spoil." (Ps. 119:162).

Instead of getting angry in a traffic jam or while waiting at the doctor's office or grocery line, try having Scripture verses on Post-It Notes™, small cards, or your phone's lock screen. that you can read and work on memorizing while you wait. The Lord will bring those verses to mind just when you need them the most! As God's word becomes your treasure, you will find that your treasure brings you joy.

Father, may we truly treasure Your word in our hearts. Grant us the power and strength through Your Holy Spirit to live out what we have learned in Your word.

REJOICING UPON RECOGNIZING THE RESURRECTED REDEEMER

It was the first day of the week, and that very evening, while the disciples were together with the doors locked for fear of the Jews, Jesus came and stood among them. "Peace be with you!" He said to them. After He had said this, He showed them His hands and His side. The disciples rejoiced[G5463] *when they saw the Lord.*

John 20:19-20

The disciples were locked inside the room where they were staying because they were afraid the Jewish leaders would have them arrested for following Jesus. They were trying to stay inconspicuous, under the radar of the religious elite by not going out among them and being holed up behind locked doors. Suddenly, Jesus was standing in front of them. He did not knock or wait for someone to ask Him the password. He just entered through the locked doors without even opening them! Jesus, the Prince of Peace, greeted them with, "Peace be with you." He was the only One who could restore peace to their trembling hearts. Jesus verified that it was He by bodily proof, voluntarily showing the disciples the nail scars in His hands and the hole in His side where the spear pierced Him. The disciples rejoiced when they realized it was truly Jesus, and He really had risen from the dead as He had told them beforehand—which they seem to have forgotten. Their extreme sorrow at the death of their Messiah, Teacher, and Friend and their fear after His crucifixion all melted away and was replaced by exuberant joy! The impossible was made possible by the power of God. Jesus was not a ghost but was standing in front of them in flesh and blood. He proved this when He invited Thomas who had not been there when He first appeared to the disciples to touch Him:

John 20:26-28 *Eight days later, His disciples were once again inside with the doors locked, and Thomas was with them. Jesus came and stood among them and said, "Peace be with you." Then Jesus said to Thomas, "Put your finger here and look at My hands. Reach out your hand and put it into My side. Stop doubting and believe." Thomas replied, "My Lord and my God!"*

We look forward to having perfected bodies when we are with the Lord someday. However, notice that Jesus chose to retain the scars of crucifixion to prove His love and His identity to His disciples. Remember that those scars were made when Jesus died in your place and mine on the cross. Reflect on the price that was paid for our salvation and thank the Lord.

Father, may we never forget the price Jesus paid to reconcile us to You! May we remember always that You resurrected Him to be the "the firstborn from the dead" (Colossians 1:18) which gives us the assurance that we, too, will be raised from the dead to live with Him forever! That is a reason to REJOICE!

You can reflect on the grace and love our Lord Jesus for us as you listen to Michael Card's powerful song "Known by the Scars" here: https://www.youtube.com/watch?v=Gr6jioscVyg

BARNABAS REJOICED BECAUSE PEOPLE WERE REDEEMED

When news of this reached the ears of the church in Jerusalem, they sent Barnabas to Antioch. When he arrived and saw the grace of God, he rejoiced^{G5463} and encouraged them all to abide in the Lord with all their hearts. Barnabas was a good man, full of the Holy Spirit and faith, and a great number of people were brought to the Lord.

Acts 11:22-24

News of what? They heard that the Good News had been preached to Gentiles in Antioch by men from Cypress and Cyrene.

> 11:23 — When he arrived and witnessed the grace of God, he rejoiced and began to encourage them. How does one witness the grace of God? By observing its fruit: people being saved, dynamic worship, forgiving spirits, peace, joy, and so forth. We encourage such grace to flourish by exhorting each other to eagerly and tenaciously serve the living God. (46)

Barnabas observed the developing Fruit of the Spirit in the believers at Antioch, and he rejoiced. He exhorted them to stay plugged into the Lord "with all their hearts." As he encouraged these new believers, even more people surrendered their lives to Jesus. Barnabas was "full of the Holy Spirit and faith." The people of Antioch were surely blessed to learn from someone with his maturity in the Lord.

Wouldn't it be great if we could be described as the writer of Acts described Barnabas? When people observe our lives, do they see us so full of the Holy Spirit that His fruit is easily seen? Do we have a reputation for being strong in faith?

Barnabas was also known as an encourager:

Acts 4:36-37 *Now Joseph, a Levite of Cyprian birth, who was also called Barnabas by the apostles (which translated means Son of Encouragement), owned a tract of land. So he sold it, and brought the money and laid it at the apostles' feet.*

Because the apostles saw the Christ-like characteristic of encouraging others, they actually gave him that nickname! What might other believers use as a nickname for us? What nickname would we like to earn—Joy, Peace-maker, Patience, Kind-hearted? Remain in Jesus, abide in His word, obey His commands, and allow the Holy Spirit to flow through you like a refreshing river. Be conscious of whether or not others see Jesus when they closely observe your life. Your actions are a more powerful testimony than your words. Be a "Barnabas" and encourage others to be full of the Holy Spirit, too!

Father, may the Fruit of the Spirit become more and more evident in our lives, so that others will truly see Jesus through us. Thank You that it is You that accomplishes this in us and not dependent upon any effort of our own other than being daily surrendered to You.

Worship with "Let Others See Jesus in You" sung by John McKay:
https://www.youtube.com/watch?v=nomNLqN9Swo

GOOD NEWS CAUSES GREAT REJOICING

"For this is what the Lord has commanded us: 'I have made you a light for the Gentiles, to bring salvation to the ends of the earth.'" When the Gentiles heard this, they rejoiced[G5463] *and glorified the word of the Lord, and all who were appointed for eternal life believed. And the word of the Lord spread throughout that region. The Jews, however, incited the religious women of prominence and the leading men of the city. They stirred up persecution against Paul and Barnabas and drove them out of their district. So they shook the dust off their feet in protest against them and went to Iconium. And the disciples were filled with joy*[G5479] *and with the Holy Spirit."*

Acts 13:47-52

Paul and Barnabas had been preaching to the Jews in Pisidian Antioch, but they rejected their message about Jesus. Therefore, they turned their attention to the Gentiles. The Gentiles rejoiced to learn about Jesus—the Jewish Messiah who had been rejected by His own people. Paul and Barnabas were the first to share but must not have been the only ones talking about Jesus because "the word of the Lord spread throughout that region." In their joyous exuberance the new Gentile believers eagerly shared the Gospel with everyone they knew. The Jews in the city were aggravated by the stir caused by Paul and Barnabas and used the leading women to incite a riot of persecution against them to drive them out of town. As Jesus had instructed the Twelve when they encountered persecution or their message was not well received, Paul and Barnabas shook the dust off their feet as they left Pisidian Antioch.

Mark 6:11 *If anyone will not welcome you or listen to you, shake the dust off your feet when you leave that place, as a testimony against them. (see also Matthew 10:14, Luke 9:5)*

Which disciples were filled with joy? Paul and Barnabas or the people who had newly become followers of Jesus? Or both? Paul and Barnabas could certainly rejoice over new brothers and sisters added to the family of God and, also, to have been counted worthy to suffer persecution because of their love for Jesus.

> 13:52 When the Holy Spirit is doing his work within you, you can experience internal peace and joy regardless of your external circumstances. (47)

Another reference material suggests that the new believers were the ones filled with "joy and the Holy Spirit:"

> 13:52 The new "disciples" left behind at Pisidian Antioch, far from being discouraged at this turn of events, were "filled with joy and with the Holy Spirit." (48)

It is highly likely that both perspectives are true. Surely the missionaries, Paul and Barnabas, were joyful and filled with the Holy Spirit. Upon believing the Good News of Jesus, the Gentile believers were inhabited by the Holy Spirit and experiencing the true joy of God's presence in their lives.

Does the presence of the Holy Spirit cause you to rejoice? Do you consider it a joy to obey God even when some people react adversely to your message?

Father, may our delight truly be found in You. May true joy be seen on our faces and reflected in our attitudes. Please grow the fruit of the Spirit "joy" within us causing it to blossom in such a way that others see You.

JOY DISTRIBUTORS

Then some men came down from Judea and were teaching the brothers, "Unless you are circumcised according to the custom of Moses, you cannot be saved." And after engaging these men in sharp debate, Paul and Barnabas were appointed, along with some other believers, to go up to Jerusalem to see the apostles and elders about this question. Sent on their way by the church, they passed through Phoenicia and Samaria, recounting the conversion of the Gentiles and bringing great joy[G5479] *to all the brothers. On their arrival In Jerusalem, they were welcomedby the church and apostles and elders, to whom they reported all that God had done through them.*

Acts 15:1-4

Paul and Barnabas were on their way to Jerusalem to talk to the church leadership about the fact that Gentiles were being converted to Christ. In the midst of this journey, Paul and Barnabas seized every opportunity to declare God's faithfulness to the Gentiles as well as the Jews. God had promised Abraham, "I will make your descendants as numerous as the stars in the sky, and I will give them all these lands, and through your offspring all nations of the earth will be blessed" (Genesis 26:4). This was also the fulfilment of what Christ had told the disciples as He ascended to Heaven after His resurrection, "But you will receive power when the Holy Spirit comes upon you, and you will be My witnesses in Jerusalem, and in all Judea and Samaria, and to the ends of the earth" (Acts 1:8). The believers along the way celebrated the conversion of the Gentiles joyfully.

Yes, Paul and Barnabas were in "full-time ministry." However, they also shared as they were traveling from point A to point B. We are all God's ministers—His ambassadors—to the world. We are to distribute the good news of Jesus Christ, the Source of our joy, as we go about our day-to-day business. An excellent example of this from more recent history is from the life of R. G. LeTourneau, the businessman who founded LeTourneau University, a Christian college. He originally thought that to be serious about one's commitment to Christ required a life of being a pastor or missionary. When he spoke to his pastor about the possibility of becoming a missionary, the pastor replied, "You know, Brother LeTourneau, God needs businessmen as well as preachers and missionaries." From that day on, LeTourneau considered God his business partner and endeavored to share his faith along the way while doing business every day. To read more about Mr. LeTourneau's life and ministry, go to https://www.wayoflife.org/reports/christian_inventor_rg_letourneau.html.

Do you distribute the joy of the gospel along your way? Do you rejoice at the salvation of one at the altar on Sunday mornings or at the reports from the mission front of conversions and baptisms? Or do you keep checking your watch because you may have to wait in a longer line at the restaurant if church runs late? We pray "Your kingdom come, Your will be done, on earth as it is in heaven" (Matthew 6:10), but do we mean it? Heaven rejoices over each sinner who surrenders to Jesus, do you?

Luke 15:7 *In the same way, I tell you that there will be more joy in heaven over one sinner who repents than over ninety-nine righteous ones who do not need to repent.*

Father, please give us a renewed excitement to share the Gospel and great rejoicing when we see people come to Jesus for salvation. Let us take joy in the things that give You pleasure. Help us to truly desire that Your will be done here and now.

JOYFUL, PATIENT, AND PERSISTENT

Be joyful[G5463] in hope[G1680], patient[G5278] in affliction, persistent[G4342] in prayer.

Romans 12:12

G1680. *elpís*; gen. elpídos, fem. noun. Hope, desire of some good with expectation of obtaining it. (49)

G5278. *hupoménō*; fut. hupomenō̂, from hupó (5259), under, and ménō (3306), to remain. To remain under, i.e., to persevere, endure, sustain, bear up under, suffer, as a load of miseries, adversities, persecutions or provocations with faith. (50)

G4342. *proskartereō* . . . used metaphorically of steadfastness and faithfulness in the outgoings of the Christian life, especially in prayer (Acts 1:14; 2:42; 6:4; Rom. 12:12; Col. 4:2). (51)

We can "be joyful in hope" because our hope is based on the promises of God, and He is faithful even when we lack faith or are unfaithful to Him.

2 Timothy 2:13 . . . *if we are faithless, He remains faithful, for He cannot deny Himself.*

What are we hoping for? What good thing do we desire? Our main hope is to be forever in the presence of the Lord, no longer besieged by sin, no more worries, no more sorrow, no more tears. We can be joyful even in the middle of this world's turmoil because our hope is based on the righteousness of Jesus and not our own ability to achieve perfection and peace. Therefore, we can also be "patient" or persevere in affliction because our hope is sure, and our faith endures:

Hebrews 11:1 *Now faith is the assurance of what we hope for and the certainty of what we do not see.*

We are "persistent"—steadfast and faithful—in prayer based on our joyful hope—our expectation of obtaining all the Lord has promised.

Look at these three commands: be joyful, be patient, be persistent. Does the promise of eternal life that begins the moment you surrender your life to the Lord stir up joy in you? Christians should be the most joy-filled people on earth. Jesus loved us enough to die in our place, and He says He has gone ahead to prepare a place for us! The Holy Spirit within us can enable us to face the trials of life patiently as we pray persistently for God's will to "be done, on earth as it is in heaven" (Matthew 6:10b). Perhaps we should use Romans 12:12 as a prayer to begin the day.

Father, help us to have joy in hoping for the day all Your promises will be fulfilled, help us to be patient when the world is particularly difficult, and help us to persist in praying that Your will be done in us.

Rejoice^G5463^ with those who rejoice^G5463^; weep with those who weep.

Romans 12:15

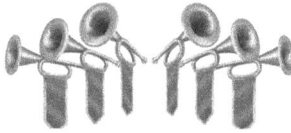

WHAT KIND OF FRIEND ARE YOU?

One day my world was falling apart.
Many burdens lay heavy upon my heart,
so I talked to Mr. Positive Attitude.
He wouldn't listen. He just sang this tune:

Get your chin up off the ground!
Don't you know Christians ain't s'posed to frown?
Don't you remember Romans 8:28?
Now...Smile! Jesus loves you and have a nice day!

I decided to visit Mrs. Suffering Saint.
Perhaps she would understand my complaint.
She listened but had no encouraging word.
As I was leaving, she sang this dirge:

We all must suffer a heavy load.
With tears we must walk down the road.
We'll find relief in the By and By.
Someday we'll have that Pie in the Sky.

Finally, I found Miss I. Really Care.
She took time to listen, and she let me share.
She let me cry but not for too long,
then taught me to sing her song:

Delight to rejoice with those who rejoice,
to praise the Lord with joyful noise.
But don't forget to weep with those who weep
and help them up the road that is steep!

JOYFULLY CLEAR A PATH
FOR YOUR BROTHER

Therefore let us stop judging one another. Instead, make up your mind not to put any stumbling block or obstacle in your brother's way. I am convinced and fully persuaded in the Lord Jesus that nothing is unclean in itself. But if anyone regards something as unclean, then for him it is unclean. If your brother is distressed by what you eat, you are no longer acting in love. Do not by your eating destroy your brother, for whom Christ died. Do not allow what you consider good, then, to be spoken of as evil. For the kingdom of God is not a matter of eating and drinking, but of righteousness, peace, and joy[G5479] *in the Holy Spirit. For whoever serves Christ in this way is pleasing to God and approved by men.*

Romans 14:13-18

The point of this passage is that the way we behave affects those with whom we are in relationship. What we do has a rippling effect to those in our sphere of influence. Our concern for our brothers and sisters in Christ should outweigh the exercise of our freedom in Christ. There are many things that are not "sin" in and of themselves that can adversely impact other believers. For example, a person may enjoy a glass of wine with a meal; but that person should consider how exercising this freedom may appear to a brother who struggles with alcoholism. If someone, as an adult, exercises his or her freedom to drink in moderation, what example or precedent may be set for their children? The Bible does not say to never drink. However, it does say:

Ephesians 5:18-20 (VOICE) *Don't drink wine excessively. The drunken path is a reckless path. It leads nowhere. Instead, let God fill you with the Holy Spirit. When you are filled with the Spirit, you are empowered to speak to each other in the soulful words of pious songs, hymns, and spiritual songs; to sing and make music with your hearts attuned to God; and to give thanks to God the Father every day through the name of our Lord Jesus the Anointed for all He has done.*

The easiest way to avoid being drunk, of course, is to not drink at all; but that is a prayerful choice each Christian must make according to his or her own convictions. An excerpt from the commentary before Romans 15 in The Voice Bible may help as you sort out your own convictions on this topic:

> Personal freedom must always give way to corporate responsibility. To put it another way, the gospel of love demands that we surrender individual liberties for the sake of our brothers and sisters. (52)

Are you conscientious about how your words and behavior may edify or cause stumbling? Are you committed to contributing to righteousness, peace, and joy among the body of believers?

Father, make us keenly aware of how our actions, especially the exercise of the freedom we have in Jesus, impact our brothers and sisters in Christ.

JOY INFUSION

I pray that God, the source of all hope, will infuse your lives with an abundance of joy[G5479] and peace in the midst of your faith so that your hope will overflow through the power of the Holy Spirit.

Romans 15:13 (VOICE)

There is no way to achieve true joy, peace, hope, and power in and of our own strength. Paul is praying that the believers in Rome depend on the power of the Holy Spirit. The Bible gives a foundation for intercessory prayer in the prayers of Paul. In the midst of my (Susan's) battle, right after the amputation of my legs, and even now, knowing that people are persistently interceding on my behalf encourages me. My current fight is to get back into my power chair on a regular basis despite back pain that radiates to my toes that aren't there (phantom pain is a grizzly bear). My desire is to make broader ripples touching my community, my city, and my world. Susie and I share in this desire to lead impactful Christian lives. We both still need to know that people are lifting us up in prayer for our personal needs as well as for the needs of Precious Jewels Ministries, Inc.

Do you know a brother or sister struggling with challenges or maybe even hopelessness? Pray the Lord will give them an infusion of joy and peace. Pray that the power of the Holy Spirit will not only renew their hope but cause it to continually overflow. Take every opportunity to be a joy in the lives of other believers. Encourage the "familyship" of faith by reminding them to turn to the Source of their joy, the Lord Jesus. This can be done in person or by text, email, snail-mail, FaceTime™, Facebook™, or whatever other social media you and your circle share. A simple "I prayed for you today" text may be more impactful than you can imagine.

Father, remind us to follow Paul's example by interceding for others and encouraging them to lean on You.

OVERFLOWING JOY

*Great is my confidence in you; great is my pride in you;
I am filled with encouragement; in all our troubles my
joy*^{G5479} *overflows.*

2 Corinthians 7:4

The Apostle Paul, who had once persecuted Christians thinking he was righteous in doing so and had stood as an approving witness to the stoning of Stephen, now had faced persecution as a believer himself. In his journeys as a missionary to proclaim Christ, he had been beaten, stoned, shipwrecked, and left for dead (see 2 Corinthians 11:16-33). However, he was still affirming the abundant joy that radiated from his heart due to his relationship with Jesus.

We are joyful that we have the opportunity to touch others' lives because of the intimate touch of Jesus in our lives. Are we happy at every moment? NO! Transparency and authenticity is difficult as we share our experiences, but it is not our story: it is HIS story being lived out through us. Therefore, we have no right to hold back the truth. We surrendered our lives to the lordship of Jesus Christ, so now our lives are His to live through us, His to guide, and His story to tell. Susan still has limited use of her hands, sleep apnea, and phantom pain, just to name a few challenges and at this writing is still "bed-found" most of the time. Susie is still recovering from major back surgery, has asthma, and has osteo-arthritis in most of her joints. We are not continuously "happy" because "happiness" depends upon circumstances. However, the joy of intimacy with our Lord remains, the commission to bring others to Him is still our delight.

The Lord has a purpose for you as well. Pray that He will show you the abundance of joy that comes from fulfilling your calling in Christ. When you discover and live the assignment God has for you, the joy you experience will overflow to others.

Father, may our joy be infectious as we tell others about Jesus!

JOYOUS GENEROSITY

Now, brothers, we want you to know about the grace that God has given the churches of Macedonia. In the terrible ordeal they suffered, their abundant joy[G5479] and deep poverty overflowed into rich generosity. For I testify that they gave according to their ability and even beyond it. Of their own accord, they earnestly pleaded with us for the privilege of sharing in this service to the saints. And not only did they do as we expected, but they gave themselves first to the Lord and then to us, because it was the will of God.

2 Corinthians 8:1-5

8:1 grace of God. The generosity of the churches of Macedonia was motivated by God's grace. Paul did not merely commend those churches for a noble human work, but instead gave the credit to God for what He did through them. churches of Macedonia. Macedonia was the northern Roman province of Greece. Paul's reference was to the churches at Philippi, Thessalonica, and Berea (cf. Acts 17:11). This was basically an impoverished province that had been ravaged by many wars and even then was being plundered by Roman authority and commerce. (53)

The Churches of Macedonia did not allow their circumstances to dictate the measure of their generosity. What enabled them to be generous despite their own poverty and affliction was their abundance of joy. In fact, they begged Paul to allow them to send a gift to the needy saints of Jerusalem.

Due to the joy of our salvation, we can still minister, trusting the Lord in the midst of our own needs. The desire to minister should be the overarching consideration, even greater than our requirements, so much so that our focus should not be on our own need. We should seek out others in need of ministry while we expectantly await the Lord's provision of our basics. When we focus on our own problems, it can be paralyzing and give us tunnel vision, taking us off of God's course for our lives. When we seek to bless others, we increase both their joy and our own. Precious Jewels Ministries, Inc. once received a small donation, under twenty dollars, from a dear Christian widow. Her life of joy has been a blessing to Susie and her family for many years. Her gift was large since she is on a fixed income. Susie knows it was motivated by love and the joy of knowing her Lord. Perhaps, the joy-filled, encouraging demeanor she demonstrates consistently is a result of blessing others. She thinks first of others' needs before considering her own.

Do you have a problem or need right now? Trust in the Lord to care for you and allow Him to care for others through you. Generosity brings joy not only to the recipient but also to the giver.

Father, help us to give from an abundance of joy even when we are in need ourselves. We have seen You bless us many times through the generosity of our brothers and sisters in Christ. Help us to be able to bless others!

THE FRUIT OF JOY

But the fruit of the Spirit is love, joy,[G5479] *peace, pa-tience, kindness, goodness, faithfulness, gentleness, and self-control. Against such things there is no law.*

Galatians 5:22-23

One evidence of being in relationship with Jesus, thus filled with the Holy Spirit, is the presence of joy. How is joy defined?

> Joy – a delight of the mind, from the consideration
> of the present or assured approaching possession of
> good. (54)

Joy is not an emotion determined by circumstances. Joy is a gift from God Himself that is eternal. This gift of un-quenchable, unconquerable joy stays dormant until and unless a person receives salvation through Jesus Christ. In believing that Jesus is the Son of God who died to pay the debt of our sin and was then raised to life by God, we receive the Holy Spirit and the joy of the Lord. Fruit takes time to be cultivated. On the TV show The Waltons™, there was an episode in which Cousin Zadok had cultivated an apple tree that produces more than one type of apple. We are a tree bearing several types of fruit—Christlike attributes. We do not instantaneously exhibit all the character qualities listed here. But the Fa-ther begins nurturing them as soon as we come to Christ. Fruit trees need water, sunlight, the right soil conditions, and proper pruning to bear the best fruit. We need to be watered with the word of God, bask in the Sonlight of Jesus, plant ourselves in a church that nourishes us, and allow God to prune away anything that would distract us from producing the Fruit of the Spirt.

Do you see these attributes, the Fruit of the Spirit in the verses above, growing in your own life, and can you spot them in others? Water your life, your fruit tree, with the word of God. Remain in the Light, Jesus. Plant yourself in a Bible teaching church family to be nourished. Be sensitive to the Father's pruning of habits and activities that draw you away from Him instead closer to Him. Pray to bear good fruit. Stay plugged into the vine, Jesus, for apart from Him you cannot bear fruit.

John 15:4-5 *Remain in Me, and I will remain in you. Just as no branch can bear fruit by itself unless it remains in the vine, neither can you bear fruit unless you remain in Me. I am the vine and you are the branches. The one who remains in Me, and I in him, will bear much fruit. For apart from Me you can do nothing.*

Father, please continue to cultivate the Fruit of the Spirit in us as we study Your word and rely on the Holy Spirit's guidance.

TO LIVE IS CHRIST: TO SPREAD HIS JOY TO OTHERS

For to me, to live is Christ, and to die is gain. But if I go on living in the body, this will mean fruitful labor for me. So what shall I choose? I do not know. I am torn between the two. I desire to depart and be with Christ, which is far better indeed.But it is more necessary for you that I remain in the body. Convinced of this, I know that I will remain and will continue with all of you for your progress and joy[G5479] in the faith, so that through my coming to you again your exultation[G2745] in Christ Jesus will resound on account of me.

Philippians 1:21-26

Evidence from the pastoral letters, confirmed by early historical testimony, indicates that Paul was released from this first Roman imprisonment and began to travel, including a trip through Macedonia (and presumably Philippi), before being reimprisoned and suffering a martyr's death. Paul's continued ministry among the Philippians would be aimed at advancing their spiritual growth and deepening their joy in the Christian faith. Believers should not be static in their faith but should grow in understanding of spiritual truth. This will increase their joy as they enter more fully into the understanding of their privileges and prospects in Christ. (55)

We must remind ourselves that Paul was writing to the Philippians while imprisoned in Rome, probably chained to a Roman soldier. Therefore, death was a real possibility in his near future. In this passage, Paul made his oft preached statement, "For to me, to live is Christ, and to die is gain" (Philippians 1:21). He knew that if the Romans executed him, he would immediately be in the presence of Jesus with no more concerns, no more thorn in the flesh, no more struggles, which would certainly be "gain". However, Paul knew that if the Lord spared his life, he would remain in service to Jesus here on earth which is what he meant by to "live is Christ." He concluded that surely God would have him remain on earth to continue his ministry of encouraging and discipling the churches. He said this would be not only for the Philippians' progress but for their joy.

As we progress in the faith, as we draw nearer to Jesus, not only are we more fruitful in our witness to others; but our joy increases exponentially. Some days we may think it would be easier to just leave here to be with Jesus. However, as long as there is breath in our bodies, God has a purpose for us here on earth. As we desire to know Jesus more and to make Him known to others, we will have the joy of fulfilling God's plan for us. We are not here to simply "bide our time" until the Lord calls us home. We are here to glorify God! Are you living up to your potential to bring people to Christ? Are you finding joy in serving Jesus here and now? Are there people you feel you need to pour into before you die? There is no better day than today. To live is Christ—to be Jesus with skin on by encouraging, teaching, and spreading joy to others.

Father, may the joy of knowing You deeper flow from us to the people we encounter day-to-day. As we grow, may we be a conduit of grace, peace, and joy.

JOYFULLY SPILLED OUT

But even if I am being poured out like a drink offering on the sacrifice and service of your faith, I am glad[G5463] and rejoice[G4796] with all of you. So you too should be glad[G5463] and rejoice[G4796] with me.

Philippians 2:17-18

(**W**hat is a drink offering?) What we do know is that the pouring out of a drink offering is a metaphor for the blood Jesus spilled on the cross. Jesus spoke to this directly in Luke 22:20 when He instituted the New Covenant. He picked up a cup of wine and said, "This cup which is poured out for you is the new covenant in My blood." Jesus' sacrifice fulfilled the need of a drink offering, His blood literally pouring out when the soldier pierced His side with a spear (John 19:34). See the article at https://www.gotquestions.org/drink-offering.html

2:17 The apostle uses a very beautiful illustration to describe the service of the Philippians and of himself. He borrows the picture from the common practice among both Jews and pagans of pouring out a drink offering or libation over a sacrifice as it was being offered. He speaks of the Philippians as the offerers. Their faith is the sacrifice. Paul himself is the drink offering. He would be happy to be poured out in martyrdom on the sacrifice and service of their faith. (56)

2:17, 18 I . . . rejoice . . . you also . . . rejoice. An attitude of mutual joy ought to accompany any sacrificial Christian service (see notes on 1:4, 18, 26; cf. 2 Cor. 7:4; Col. 1:24; 1 Thess. 3:9). (57)

The Apostle Paul who had been a persecutor of Christians, completely turned around after his encounter with Jesus on the Damascus Road (Acts 9:1-19). After his conversion to Christianity, Paul poured his entire being into sharing the Good News about Jesus, teaching new converts, and encouraging the church through letters. Paul was being poured out continually, but in this verse may have been referring to the prospect of martyrdom. The drink offering was completely "spilled out" upon the sacrifice on the altar. How could Paul's being completely poured out—martyred—be an occasion for gladness and rejoicing? Martyr can also be translated "witness". Dying because of service to God is certainly a powerful witness of confidence in Jesus. As John MacArthur pointed out, we should celebrate sacrificial service. The word for "rejoice" in the Greek could be translated "to congratulate". We should congratulate each other for being faithful in our service to the Lord. Paul was willing to serve God and his brothers and sisters in Christ no matter what the cost. As the article on www.gotquestions.org pointed out, Jesus's blood could be considered a drink offering poured out on His sacrifice of Himself as the final sacrificial Lamb to satisfy the penalty for our sin.

How far are you willing to go in serving God? Not all are called to vocational ministry, but all believers are ministers. Are you willing to sacrifice time normally spent in leisure pursuits to be Jesus with skin on to help a neighbor? Are you willing to give up what you want to do to follow God's purpose for you? God's choice is always the better choice but may not feel that way initially.

Father, thank You for sending Your own Son as a sacrifice in our place. Help us to be willing and infuse us with Your strength to live our lives being spilled out and used up for Your glory.

Follow the link below to listen to a beautiful song about sacrifice, the sacrifice of the woman who broke the vessel to anoint Jesus for burial and the sacrifice of Jesus who poured out Himself on the cross to bring us new life with Him forever. Allison Durham Spear and the Gaither Homecoming Friends singing "Broken and Spilled Out." https://www.youtube.com/watch?v=xUi3whcg8Ww

Finally, my brothers, rejoice^{G5463} in the Lord. It is no trouble for me to write the same things to you again, and it is a safeguard for you.

Philippians 3:1

rejoice in the Lord. Cf. 4:4. Paul's familiar theme throughout the epistle which has already been heard in chaps. 1, 2. This, however, is the first time he adds "in the Lord," which signifies the sphere in which the believers' joy exists—a sphere unrelated to the circumstances of life, but related to an unassailable, unchanging relationship to the sovereign Lord. (58)

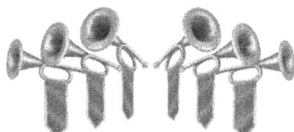

REJOICE IN THE LORD

Authentic, audacious, irrepressible joy
can only be experienced "in the Lord."
We may only find temporary happiness
in the things we buy and hoard.
Our joy is not found in accomplishments;
we must place no confidence in our deeds.
As Paul said, our achievements are rubbish
and cannot fulfill our deepest needs.
Only through trust in the Lord Jesus
can we find righteousness, peace, and joy.

His dying in our place upon the cross
is the only sacrifice we can employ.
The gift of grace Christ purchased,
given freely to all who believe,
gives us unchangeable, unassailable access
to God through the salvation we receive.
Our joy is not marred by circumstance.
It cannot be taken away.
We simply need to walk in His light
and make the choice to rejoice each day.

CHOICE TO REJOICE ALWAYS

Rejoice in the Lord always. I will say it again: Rejoice!
Philippians 4:4

> The command to rejoice can always be obeyed, even in the middle of conflict, adversity, and deprivation, because joy rests not on favorable circumstances, but "in the Lord." (59)

I (Susan) have found this to be true in my own journey. I had to lie virtually flat on my back for four-and-a-half years due to a dislocated knee and the necrotic ulcers on my legs and feet. Turning was excruciating because of the need to put a brace on each leg beforehand, as well as two straps around both legs to enable the legs to move in tandem. The side I have the most balance on is also the side to which my pelvis is swept—a dislocation common in people with cerebral palsy—causing pain when my body weight is on that side. After turning, the braces would have to be removed, inflicting great pain as scabs that had stuck to the braces would come off. However, I could still rejoice by knowing that in the midst of all these difficulties, the Lord is by my side, constantly present.

The struggles of this life, even though they may feel permanent, are only temporary; but the glory of heaven is eternal.

2 Corinthians 4:17 (VOICE) *You see, the short-lived pains of this life are creating for us an eternal glory that does not compare to anything we know here.*

Perhaps you are experiencing chronic pain. Maybe you struggle financially. You may have been betrayed by a friend or abandoned by your spouse. Loneliness may encompass you at times. No matter what challenges you face today, you can make a choice to rejoice by remembering all the Lord has done and will do for you in this life and forever.

Father, help us to choose joy daily as we remember and reflect on all You have done for us and the promise of our forever home with You!

JOY AND THANKFULNESS
NO MATTER WHAT

Dedicated to Betsy Hall, Elizabeth Polson, Kitty Huber, and Sandra Tarno

Rejoice[G5463] *always and delight in your faith; be unceasing and persistent in prayer; in every situation [no matter what the circumstances] be thankful and continually give thanks to God; for this is the will of God for you in Christ Jesus.*

1Thessalonians 5:16-18 (AMP)

At this very moment, I am in pain. My foot that is no longer there is having spasms, phantom pain. We tend to think of rejoicing as a feeling, but it is not. It is bound up in relationship, my relationship to our heavenly Father that I am devoted to and committed to no matter what. Joy is possible because God loves me and chose me when I was unworthy because of sin. I wouldn't even have the capacity to love Him unless He loved me first (1 John 4:19). I can give thanks to God when I pray, even when I am in pain, because He is faithful. I have trusted Jesus, surrendered my life to Him; and thanksgiving is His will and destiny for me. What the Lord instructs me to do, He empowers me to do through the Holy Spirit within me.

The Holy Spirit can give you the ability to rejoice and praise the Lord even during struggles. Make a conscientious effort to thank the Lord even while you are hurting. Obedience to the commands in the verses above will help you to overcome whatever challenges you face.

Lord, in obedience and by the power of Your Holy Spirit within me, I thank You for the phantom pain, the spasms, the sleep apnea, and all the challenges Cerebral Palsy gives my earth-suit. Thank you for giving the calm assurance of joy deep within, even during the times of greatest struggle.

JOYFUL ACCEPTANCE

Remember the early days that you were in the light. In those days, you endured a great conflict in the face of suffering. Sometimes you were publicly exposed to ridicule and persecution; at other times you were partners with those who were so treated. You sympathized with those in prison and joyfully[G5479] accepted the confiscation of your property, knowing that you yourselves had a better and permanent possession.

Hebrews 10:32-34

The human writer of Hebrews, under the inspiration of the Holy Spirit, was encouraging believers who were being persecuted for their faith even to the confiscation or destruction of their homes. They were commended for "counting it all joy" (James 1:2) when they faced these trials. Most of us who live in the United States of America have been blessed to not face persecution of this magnitude, but our brothers and sisters in many countries encounter it daily. Pastors are killed, leaving behind their spouses and children. Many who have been beaten have had the grace to forgive and even return to witness to those who harmed them. You may read their stories of joy in the middle of loss at www. persecution.com. They have this peace and joy because they know they are citizens of Heaven and that Jesus is preparing their eternal home:

John 14:1-6 *"Do not let your hearts be troubled. You be-*

lieve in God; believe in Me as well. In My Father's house are many rooms. If it were not so, would I have told you that I am going there to prepare a place for you? And if I go and prepare a place for you, I will come back and welcome you into My presence, so that you also may be where I am. You know the way to the place where I am going." "Lord," said Thomas, "we do not know where You are going, so how can we know the way?" Jesus answered, "I am the way and the truth and the life. No one comes to the Father except through Me."

Ask yourself whether or not you have the confidence in Christ to face persecution with joyful acceptance. If the answer is no, honestly ask yourself if you have ever surrendered your life to the Lord Jesus as your Savior and Lord. If you are certain of your salvation but still concerned about your ability to face persecution joyfully, ask the Lord for His strength, study His word, and maybe discuss your doubts with you pastor or Bible Study leader.

Father, we trust in Your ability to give us the strength to face persecution for our faith if and when the time comes. Thank You in advance for the perseverance and joy You will give us.

BE A JOY TO YOUR LEADERS

Obey your leaders and submit to them, for they watch over your souls as those who must give an account. To this end, allow them to lead with joy^{G5479} and not with grief, for that would be of no advantage to you.

Hebrews 13:17

After a very significant health scare, the Lord spoke to me (Susan) and said that I needed to fight because He had a good future, hope, and a plan for me according to His word:

Jeremiah 29:11 *For I know the plans I have for you, declares the LORD, plans to prosper you and not to harm you, to give you a future and a hope.*

Part of the exhortation that He gave me was that His ministers were the forgotten part—the most underserved people—of the body of Christ. Ministers need ministry in as great or greater measure than their congregations. They are constantly meeting the needs of others and often neglecting themselves. Congregations often forget this fact about their leaders. The members of the church see them at their best in the pulpit, while under the power of the Holy Spirit, or in their pastoral role at weddings, bedsides, and funerals. They do not see the humanity, the daily trials in their pastors' lives. Pastors are often lonely for close friendships, mostly due to the difficulty of carving out time. Many church members expect the pastor to be available 24/7, which leaves little time for recreation or relationships with family and/or friends. We expect pastors to live up to a higher standard, as we should; but we also need to remember that they are humans saved by grace just as we are.

Have you ever written a note of encouragement to your pastor or other church staff? Before you criticize their actions, do you also recognize the positive things in their leadership? Before you underscore their weaknesses, do you highlight their strengths? Be a joy rather than a burden to your leaders.

Father, help us to be faithful to the mission You gave us to minister to other ministers. Help us to pray consistently for them, to send them encouraging notes, and to bless them in other ways You reveal to us.

COUNT IT ALL JOY

James, a servant of God and of the Lord Jesus Christ, To the twelve tribes of the Dispersion G1290: Greetings. Consider it pure joy ^{G5479}, my brothers, when you encounter trials of many kinds, because you know that the testing of your faith develops perseverance. Allow perseverance to finish its work, so that you may be mature and complete, not lacking anything.

James 1:1-3

G1290 *diasporá*, dee-as-por-ah'; from G1289; dispersion, i.e. (specially and concretely) the (converted) Israelite resident in Gentile countries:—(which are) scattered (abroad). (60)

James 1:1 James is most likely the brother of Jesus. More specifically, since Jesus was virgin born, James was his half-brother. In Acts this same James appears as the leader of the Jerusalem church (Acts 15:13ff.; 21:18). He describes himself as "a servant of God and of the Lord Jesus Christ." This word designates a slave, the rightful property of one's master, though it does not necessarily carry the degrading connotation attached to the word today. James was proud to belong—body and soul—to God and to Jesus Christ. The letter is addressed to "the twelve tribes," a designation intended to identify the readers as Jews. They were not residents of Palestine but were "scattered among the nations" as part of the Jewish Dispersion. James's later designation of his readers as "believers in our glorious Lord Jesus Christ" (2:1) makes it clear that he means Christian Jews. It is probable that the recipients were the members of the Jerusalem church who had been driven out of Jerusalem at the time of Stephen's martyrdom (Ac 8:1, 4; 11:19-20). If so, James had formerly been their spiritual leader and he was writing them with rightful spiritual authority and with full knowledge of their needs. (61)

Joy, even during the trials and tests, can be ours if we remember that God is in complete control. God permits difficulties for the main purpose of shaping our character into the likeness of Christ (Romans 8:29). I (Susan) have not been able to do weight bearing exercise since about the age of twelve due to my cerebral palsy and its complications. Because of this, I have osteoporosis. My bones are not very strong. Just as our bones need the pressure of weight-bearing exercise in order to strengthen and increase their density, we need tests of our faith in order to build up our spiritual houses. Our Father knows that we need small trials along the way in preparation for greater tests of faith. There is joy in the ability God gives us to stand confidently firm as we clothe ourselves in His armor.

Ephesians 6:10-18 *Finally, be strong in the Lord and in His mighty power. Put on the full armor of God, so that you can make your stand against the devil's schemes. For our struggle is not against flesh and blood, but against the rulers, against the authorities, against the powers of this world's darkness, and against the spiritual forces of evil in the heavenly realms. Therefore take up the full armor of God, so that when the day of evil comes, you will be able to stand your ground, and having done everything, to stand. Stand firm then, with the belt of truth buckled around your waist, with the breastplate of righteousness arrayed, and with your feet fitted with the readiness of the gospel of peace. In addition to all this, take up the shield of faith, with which you can extinguish all the flaming arrows of the evil one. And take the helmet of salvation and the sword of the Spirit, which is the word of God. Pray in the Spirit at all times, with every kind of prayer and petition. To this end, stay alert with all perseverance in your prayers for all the saints.*

Are you experiencing trials? Find joy in knowing that the Lord is using them to make you stronger and more like Jesus.

Father, we thank You that the trials in our lives teach us to depend more completely on You and strengthen our faith. Help us remember that times of testing can deepen our relationship with You when we fully rely on You. Help us to be joyful even in the middle of the tests and trials.

*Though you have not seen Him, you love Him; and
though you do not see Him now, you believe in Him and
rejoice[G21] with an inexpressible and glorious joy[G5479] . . .*

1 Peter 1:8

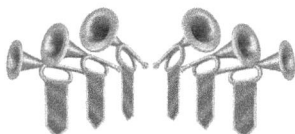

JOY INEXPRESSIBLE

The faith that leads to salvation,
complete trust in Jesus Christ
even though I've never seen Him,
has completely transformed my life.
I now have joy inexpressible
and life abundant and free
because of the love of my Savior
who gave His life for me.
Then He became the firstborn
of those who will rise from the grave,
for all who believe in and trust Him
He will irrevocably save.
I rejoice that He is now with me,
His Holy Spirit teaching and guiding.
But this cannot possibly compare to the joy
when forever with Him I'll be abiding.

INEXPRESSIBLE JOY

Though you have not seen Him, you love Him; and though you do not see Him now, you believe in Him and rejoice^{G21} with an inexpressible^{G412} and glorious joy,^{G5479} now that you are receiving the goal of your faith, the salvation of your souls.

1 Peter 1:8-9

G412. *aneklálētos*; gen. aneklalétou, masc.–fem., neut. aneklálēton, adj. from the priv. a (1), without, and eklaléō (1583), to utter. Unutterable, inexpressible (1 Pet. 1:8). (62)

The Apostle Peter is writing to people who never saw Jesus in the flesh but have instead come to know Him by being drawn by the Holy Spirit through the ministry of His apostles. The Holy Spirit is the third person of the Trinity, the God-Head. As the Holy Spirit is an equal member of the Trinity, He should not be referred to as "it.' He is the One who beckons people to surrender to the Lord, indwells believers, and clarifies God's word to them as they study. Just as Jesus is equal with the Father, the Holy Spirit is equal with Father God and Jesus as well. It is by the work of the Holy Spirit that these people could know Jesus and rejoice in Him even though they had never met Him as a man on earth. They were speechless at the wonder of having a personal, intimate relationship with the Lord Jesus Christ.

Have you experienced the astonishment of knowing almighty God personally? Even though "all have sinned and fall short of the glory of God" (Romans 3:23), He still desires to save people for Himself. Jesus died to pay the price of our sin for "the wages of sin is death" (Romans 6:23), and now He offers us the gift of God which is eternal life.

Romans 6:23 *For the wages of sin is death, but the gift of God is eternal life in Christ Jesus our Lord.*

Have you surrendered to the Holy Spirit's tug on your life and accepted this gift of salvation? If not, why wait? Experience true, complete, lasting joy now! Turn to the "Jewels of Salvation" toward the back of this book to learn more about becoming a follower of the Lord Jesus.

Father, words are inadequate to express the pure joy a relationship with Jesus brings us. Having Your Holy Spirit living in us enables us to experience this joy even during life's most difficult struggles. Thank You for the gift of joy!

Worship with Steven Moctezuma singing "Holy Spirit, Thou Art Welcome:"
https://www.youtube.com/watch?v=PP8oQtmY8QQ

REJOICE TO SHARE IN CHRIST'S SUFFERINGS

Beloved, do not be surprised at the fiery trial that has come upon you, as though something strange were happening to you. But rejoice[G5463] *that you share in the sufferings of Christ, so that you may be overjoyed*[G21] *at the revelation of His glory.If you are insulted for the name of Christ, you are blessed, because the Spirit of glory and of God rests on you.*

1 Peter 4:12-14

4:12 the fiery trial. Peter probably wrote this letter shortly before or after the burning of Rome, and at the beginning of the horrors of a 200-year period of Christian persecution. Peter explains that 4 attitudes are necessary in order to be triumphant in persecution: 1) expect it (v. 12); 2) rejoice in it (vv. 13, 14); 3) evaluate its cause (vv. 15–18); and 4) entrust it to God (v. 19). some strange thing happened. "Happened" means "to fall by chance." A Christian must not think that his persecution is something that happened accidentally. God allowed it and designed it for the believer's testing, purging, and cleansing. (63)

Peter was writing to Christians who were facing extreme persecution under the rule of the pyromaniac, Nero.

Nero's use of Christians as human torches to light

his evening garden parties is well documented. Ultimately, it is the brutality inflicted on the early Christians for which Nero is best remembered. *https://www.gotquestions.org/who-was-Nero.html*

Yet, he admonishes them to "rejoice" to share in the sufferings of Christ. Trials are not "happenstance." They are allowed by God to suit His purposes and to ultimately bring Him glory. The Apostle Paul shared Peter's conviction that suffering because of following Jesus was a blessing and a cause for rejoicing. Paul even intentionally sought the level of intimacy with Jesus that would put him in position to share in His sufferings:

Philippians 3:10 (AMPC) *[For my determined purpose is] that I may know Him [that I may progressively become more deeply and intimately acquainted with Him, perceiving and recognizing and understanding the wonders of His Person more strongly and more clearly], and that I may in that same way come to know the power outflowing from His resurrection [which it exerts over believers], and that I may so share His sufferings as to be continually transformed [in spirit into His likeness even] to His death . . .*

Having shared in Christ's sufferings will bring believers to exceeding joy "at the revelation of His glory"—when Jesus returns. Suffering persecution is a proof that the Holy Spirit rests, resides, dwells in the believer. As we obey the promptings of the Holy Spirit, we will be set apart more and more from the ways of the world. That difference is what singles out believers for persecution whether it be insults, loss of employment, or even physical abuse. Jesus expressed this concept of rejoicing when we suffer at the end of the Beatitudes:

Matthew 5:11-12 *Blessed are you when people insult you, persecute you, and falsely say all kinds of evil against you because of Me. Rejoice and be glad, because great is your reward in heaven; for in the same way they persecuted the prophets before you.*

We may not be facing persecution to the point of death, but we are sometimes maligned because of our faith. Rather than being discouraged, we should actually be glad Jesus counted us worthy to share in His sufferings. Persecution is an indication that we are doing something right because it is riling up the Enemy who is pitting people against us.

Father, help us to rejoice when we face trials due to our faith.

THE GREAT JOY OF SPIRITUAL CHILDREN

The elder, To the beloved Gaius, whom I love in the truth: Beloved, I pray that in every way you may prosper and enjoy good health, as your soul also prospers. For I was overjoyed^{G5463} when the brothers came and testified about your devotion to the truth, in which you continue to walk. I have no greater joy^{G5479} than to hear that my children are walking in the truth.

3 John 1:1-4

Some folks had come from the church where Gaius was a member and had told John that the "truth" was in him (3 John 3). That is, Gaius was learning and walking in the truth. What a tremendous report to receive about a Christian! So, John says, "I have no greater joy than to hear that my children walk in truth" (4). Notice the emphasis on "truth." The most important quality of the Christian faith is that it is true. The reference to "my children" (4) indicates that John had won Gaius to the Lord. John, the faithful pastor, was filled with joy upon receiving a good report about one of his converts. (64)

Just as our biological parents are pleased when their children have integrity and bring honor to their family, the Apostle John was glad to find those whom he had taught continuing to follow his teaching and standing in the truth of Jesus Christ. Similarly, those who have led someone to the Lord or discipled—mentored—them in studying the Bible rejoice when their spiritual children are living by godly precepts. While Susan was having a procedure to install a permanent med port rather than having to have multiple attempts to start an IV during hospitalizations, I (Susie) was sitting in the waiting room with Susan's former pastor and his wife. A nurse with whom Susan and I had shared the story of God's work in our lives the night before the amputation surgery came in because she was showing another family where to wait. She expressed concern because she thought perhaps something had gone wrong, and I reassured her that this was just a procedure Susan had requested to have done while she was in the hospital. The nurse then proceeded to thank me profusely and tell me to thank Susan for ministering God's word to her and other care providers while she was in their care. In fact, she said that we had started a revival on the fifth floor! She said the Lord had really used our words to convict and encourage her. I noticed Susan's former pastor of Restoration Church beaming as he listened to this conversation. Susan's continual ministry brought Brother Doug White, as her mentor, great joy at that moment.

Is your life bringing joy to those who have invested in your spiritual growth? If you have walked with the Lord for a long while, are you taking time to give of yourself and your experience with Him to others? If you are, then you will know the great joy of seeing them continuing in faith and standing in the truth.

Father, we rejoice when those we have encouraged in the faith continue to serve You with gladness. Thank You for allowing us to see how You have used us in others' lives. Thank You for the privilege and joy of being discipled and discipling others.

JOY IN THE LIGHT OF HIS GLORY

Now to the One who can keep you upright and plant you firmly in His presence—clean, unmarked, and joy-ful[G20] *in the light of His glory— to the one and only God, our Savior, through Jesus the Anointed our Lord, be glory and greatness and might and authority; just as it has been since before He created time, may it continue now and into eternity. Amen.*

Jude 1:24-25 (VOICE)

G20. *agallíasis*; gen. agalliáseōs, fem. noun from agalliáō (21), to exult. Exultation, exuberant joy. Not found in Gr. writers but often meaning joy, exultation (Sept.: Ps. 30:5; 45:15; 65:12, rejoicing with song, dancing. See Ps. 126:2, 6); great joy (Ps. 45:7; 51:8, 12). In the NT, joy, gladness, rejoicing (Luke 1:14, 44; Acts 2:46; Heb. 1:9 from Ps. 45:7, oil of gladness with which guests were anointed at feasts, where used as an emblem of the highest honors [cf. Jude 1:24]). (65)

If we are clean and unmarked, which we are by the grace of God through Jesus's death on the cross, we are joyful. We are confident because of what Jesus has done. The assurance that Jesus fulfilled His purposes—living a perfect life as the complete God-Man and giving Himself as a sacrifice in our place—provides us the freedom to live joyfully while fulfilling our God-given purposes. When we dwell with Christ in our heavenly home, our bodies as well as our souls, will be pristine. All scars—physical, emotional, and spiritual—will be erased. Even now, as we anticipate that day, we can rejoice because we have been anointed with the oil of gladness!

Pursue joy on a daily basis. Remind yourself of the glory, greatness, might, and authority of the One you serve. As the Apostle Paul wrote to the church at Ephesus:

Ephesians 3:20-21 *Now to Him who is able to do immeasurably more than all we ask or imagine, according to His power that is at work within us, to Him be the glory in the church and in Christ Jesus throughout all generations, forever and ever. Amen.*

Father, our ability to stand before You "clean, unmarked, and joyful" was purchased for us on the cross by Your Son, Jesus Christ. His blood was the soap of Your love to cleanse us from all unrighteousness. When we are right with You, we can live in joy. Thank you for enabling us to live joyful lives now and for eternity.

Worship with the Gaither Vocal Band singing "Center of My Joy" acapella: https://www.youtube.com/watch?v=y44bzd6M-P8

JEWELS OF SALVATION

❖ *Romans 3:22-24 And this righteousness from God comes through faith in Jesus Christ to all who believe. There is no distinction, **for all have sinned and fall short of the glory of God** and are justified freely by His grace through the redemption that is in Christ Jesus.*

Everyone on earth has sinned. Sin is both doing things that go against what God tells us to do in the Bible and failing to do the good things He instructs us to do. This failure brings the wrath of God on us, and Jesus is the **only way** to make peace with God. John 14:6 "Jesus answered, 'I am the way and the truth and the life. No one comes to the Father except through Me.'"

❖ *Romans 6:20-23 For when you were slaves to sin, you were free of obligation to righteousness. What fruit did you reap at that time from the things of which you are now ashamed? The outcome of those things is death. But now that you have been set free from sin and have become slaves to God, the fruit you reap leads to holiness, and the outcome is eternal life. **For the wages of sin is death, but the gift of God is eternal life in Christ Jesus our Lord.***

The punishment for sin is death. The official term

is "substitutionary atonement" which simply means you were sentenced to the death penalty, but Jesus volunteered to die on the cross in your place in order for you to be set free. Jesus died a painful death to redeem you from slavery to sin and spare you from the wrath of the righteous, Holy God.

❖ *Romans 5:6-8 For at just the right time, while we were still powerless, Christ died for the ungodly. Very rarely will anyone die for a righteous man, though for a good man someone might possibly dare to die.* **But God proves His love for us in this: While we were still sinners, Christ died for us.**

Jesus died while we were still sinners. "For God so loved the world that **He gave His one and only Son**, that everyone who believes in Him shall not perish but have eternal life." John 3:16.

❖ *Romans 10:8-10 But what does it say? "The word is near you; it is in your mouth and in your heart," that is, the word of faith we are proclaiming: that* **if you confess with your mouth, "Jesus is Lord," and believe in your heart that God raised Him from the dead, you will be saved.** *For with your heart you believe and are justified, and with your mouth you confess and are saved.*

1 Corinthians 15:3-4 "For what I received I passed

on to you as of first importance: that Christ died for our sins according to the Scriptures, that He was buried, that He was raised on the third day according to the Scriptures . . ." If you believe that Jesus is the Son of God who died for you and was raised to life, then trust in—rely on—Him to save you from the wrath of God, you can belong to Jesus.

❖ *Romans 10:11-13 It is just as the Scripture says: "Anyone who believes in Him will never be put to shame." For there is no difference between Jew and Greek: The same Lord is Lord of all, and gives richly to all who call on Him, for,* **"Everyone who calls on the name of the Lord will be saved."**

How do you become a member of the family of God? Pray—talk to God admitting that you cannot be good enough because you could *never* perfectly obey all His commands. Tell Him you trust that Jesus died on the cross to save you from slavery to sin and the wrath of God. Ask God to place His Holy Spirit in you and change you from the inside out. Thank Him for giving you life in His presence forever.

BELIEVER'S BENEFITS

The obvious benefit of trusting in Jesus, the Son of God who died for you and was raised from the grave to return to the right hand of His Father, and surrendering your life to him, is that instead of spending eternity separated from God and all that is good you will live in His presence in complete peace and joy. However, those who become the Lord's children by relying on Jesus gain many other things in this current life on earth. Here are a few:

❖　　Lord, we thank you for freeing us from slavery to sin and providing a way to flee temptation! Romans 6:6 "We know that our old self was crucified with Him so that the body of sin might be rendered powerless, that we should no longer be slaves to sin." This does not mean that a believer will never sin again. It means he/she now has a choice to tap into the Holy Spirit's power to resist the urge to give in to temptation. "No temptation has seized you except what is common to man. And God is faithful; He will not let you be tempted beyond what you can bear. But when you are tempted, He will also provide an escape, so that you can stand up under it" (1 Corinthians 10:13).

❖　　Lord, thank You that nothing can separate us from Your love! "For I am convinced that neither death nor life, neither angels nor principalities, neither the present nor the future, nor any powers, neither height nor depth, nor anything else in all creation, will be able to separate us from the love of God that is in Christ Jesus our Lord" (Romans 8:38-39).

❖   Lord, thank You that our salvation is secure and cannot be lost! John 10:27-29 "My sheep listen to My voice; I know them, and they follow Me. I give them eternal life, and they will never perish. No one can snatch them out of My hand. My Father who has given them to Me is greater than all. No one can snatch them out of My Father's hand."

❖   Lord thank you for empowering us to do whatever You call us to do! Philippians 4:13 (AMP) "I can do all things [which He has called me to do] through Him who strengthens and empowers me [to fulfill His purpose—I am self-sufficient in Christ's sufficiency; I am ready for anything and equal to anything through Him who infuses me with inner strength and confident peace.]

❖   Lord, thank You for giving us brothers and sisters all over the world! "Respect everyone, and love the family of believers." 1 Peter 2:17a (NLT).

DICTIONARY OF "SUSANISMS"

Bed-found – This is preferred over "bed-bound" because Susan is not chained to her bed, but these days it is usually where Susan is found.

CareGIVER – Caregivers take care of people. Caretakers maintain houses, buildings, or cemeteries! Susie is my caregiver, and I am hers!

Familyship – The family of God. We prefer "familyship" over "fellowship" because, obviously, we are not all fellows.

Framily – Friends who have become family because of our mutual love for Jesus, our brothers and sisters in Christ which may include our biological family as well.

Full-weight - Susan is not "dead weight" when we lift her because she is very much alive! We are simply bearing her full weight because she cannot assist us.

Remnants – Susan does not call her shortened legs "stumps," because stumps are something you put in a woodchipper. Her legs are "remnants" because Jesus saves and returns for the remnant.

Tater – This is Susan's nickname or job description for Susie. It is short for facilitator because Susie facilitates many things for her.

Finally, PLEASE do ***not*** refer to Susan as an invalid. She is not IN-valid. Here is her description of herself:

I AM UNIQUELY FIT FOR HIS SERVICE: A DIVINELY DESIGNED PRESENTATION!

INDEX OF SCRIPTURE REFERENCES

NOTES

1.   Lockyear, Herbert, All the Men of the Bible, (Zondervan, 1988, 2006) as quoted on www.biblegateway.com

2.   Gardner, Paul D., ed. New International Encyclopedia of Bible Characters: The Complete Who's Who in the Bible, (Zondervan, 2001). As quoted on www.biblegateway.com

3.   Sproul, R. C. ESV Reformation Study Bible, (Reformation Trust Publishing of Ligonier Ministries, 2021).

4.   Baker, Warren and Carpenter, Eugene, eds., The Complete Word Study Dictionary: Old Testament, (Chattanooga, TN: AMG Publishers, 2003).

5.   MacDonald, William, Believer's Bible Commentary, (Thomas Nelson, 2016).

6.   Hindson, E. and Mitchell, Daniel R. eds. King James Version Commentary, (Zondervan, 2010).

7.   Barker, Kenneth L. and. Kohlenberger, John R III, eds. Expositor's Bible Commentary (Abridged Edition): Old Testament, (Zondervan, 2004).

8.   Sproul, R. C. note on 1 Chronicles 12:38-40

9.   Strong, James, The New Strong's Exhaustive Concordance of the Bible, (Thomas Nelson, 2009).

10. Baker, Warren and Carpenter, Eugene, eds., on H1995.

10.   Baker, Warren and Carpenter, Eugene, eds., on H1995. 11. Strong, James, on H974

12. Baker, Warren and Carpenter, Eugene, eds. On H1875

13. Baker, Warren and Carpenter, Eugene, eds. On H1245

14. MacArthur, John, NKJV MacArthur Study Bible, 2nd Edition, (Thomas Nelson, 1997, 2006, 2019), as quoted on www.biblegateway.com

15. MacArthur, John, on Nehemiah 8:10-12

16. Bridges, Jerry, The Fruitful Life, The Overflow of God's Love Through You, (Navpress, 2006).

17. Webster, Noah, The American Dictionary of the English Language, 1828. as found at https://webstersdictionary1828.com/

18. MacArthur, John, on Psalm 16:10

19. Sproul, R.C. on Psalm 20:1

20. Sproul, R.C. on Psalm 21:2

21. MacDonald, William, on Psalm 21:4

22. Barker, Kenneth L. and. Kohlenberger, John R III, eds. On Psalm 27:6

23. Strong, James, on H7440

24. Strong, James, on H8643

25. Strong, James, on H5102

26. Webster, Noah, on HOPE

27. Webster, Noah, on INEFFABLE

28. Strong, James, on H7321

29. Spence-Jones, H. D. M. (Henry Donald Maurice), 1836-1917, editor. The Pulpit Commentary. (New York : London :Anson D.F. Randolph; Kegan Paul, Trench, 1883).

30. Barker, Kenneth L. and. Kohlenberger, John R III, eds. On Psalm 66:4

31. MacArthur, John, on Psalm 67:1-7

32. Strong, James, on H5970

33. MacArthur, John, on Psalm 87:1-7

34. MacArthur, John, on Psalm 87:7

35 MacArthur, John, on Psalm 90:1-17

36   Baker, Warren and Carpenter, Eugene, eds. On H2617

37. MacArthur, John, on Psalm 96:13

38 MacArthur, John, on Psalm 98:4

39. MacArthur, John, on Psalm 105:42-45

40. Evans, Tony, The Tony Evans Study Bible, (Holman, 2019).

41. Barker, Kenneth L. and. Kohlenberger, John R III, eds. On Luke 1:13-15

42. Barker, Kenneth L. and. Kohlenberger, John R III, eds. On Luke 1:13

43. Zodhiates, Spiros, ed., The Complete Word Study Dictionary: New Testament (Chattanooga, TN: AMG Publishers, 2000).

44. Evans, Tony, on Luke 10:21

45. MacArthur, John, NKJV MacArthur Study Bible, 2nd Edition, (Thomas Nelson, 1997, 2006, 2019), as quoted on www.biblegateway.com

46. Stanley, Charles, Charles F. Stanley Life Principles Daily Bible, (Thomas Nelson, 2011).

47. Evans, Tony, on Acts 13:52

48. Barker, Kenneth L. and. Kohlenberger, John R III, eds., on Acts 13:52

49. Zodhiates, Spiros, on G1680.

50. Zodhiates, Spiros, G5278.

51. Zodhiates, Spiros, G4342.

52. VOICE Bible (Ecclesia Bible Society. 2008). Note on Romans 15.

53. MacArthur, John, on 2 Corinthians 8:1.

54. Webster, Noah, definition of Joy.

55. Barker, Kenneth L. and. Kohlenberger, John R III, eds. On Philippians 1:21-26

56. MacDonald, William, on Philippians 2:17.

57. MacArthur, John, on Philippians 2:17-18.

58. MacArthur, John, on Philippians 3:1.

59. Sproul, R.C., on Philippians 4:4.

60. Strong, James, on G1290.

61. Barker, Kenneth L. and. Kohlenberger, John R III, eds. On James 1:1.

62. Zodhiates, Spiros, on G412

63. MacArthur, John, on 1 Peter 4:12.

64. Vines, Jerry, Vines' Expository Bible Notes, (Thomas Nelson, 2020), as quoted at www.biblegateway.com.

65. Zodhiates, Spiros, on G20.

BIBLIOGRAPHY

Baker, Warren and Carpenter, Eugene, eds., The Complete Word Study Dictionary: Old Testament, (Chattanooga, TN: AMG Publishers, 2003).

Barker, Kenneth L. and. Kohlenberger, John R III, eds. Expositor's Bible Commentary (Abridged Edition): Old Testament, (Zondervan, 2004).

Bridges, Jerry, The Fruitful Life, The Overflow of God's Love Through You, (Navpress, 2006).

Evans, Tony, The Tony Evans Study Bible, (Holman, 2019).

Gardner, Paul D., ed. New International Encyclopedia of Bible Characters: The Complete Who's Who in the Bible, (Zondervan, 2001).

Hindson, E. and Mitchell, Daniel R. eds. King James Version Commentary, (Zondervan, 2010).

Lockyear, Herbert, All the Men of the Bible, (Zondervan, 1988, 2006) as quoted on www.biblegateway.com

MacArthur, John, NKJV MacArthur Study Bible, 2nd Edition, (Thomas Nelson, 1997, 2006, 2019), as quoted on www.biblegateway.com

MacDonald, William, Believer's Bible Commentary, (Thomas Nelson, 2016).

Spence-Jones, H. D. M. (Henry Donald Maurice), 1836-1917, editor. The Pulpit Commentary. (New York : London :Anson D.F. Randolph; Kegan Paul, Trench, 1883). As quoted at:
www.biblehub.com

Sproul, R. C. ESV Reformation Study Bible, (Reformation Trust Publishing of Ligonier Ministries, 2021).

Stanley, Charles, Charles F. Stanley Life Principles Daily Bible, (Thomas Nelson, 2011).

Strong, James, The New Strong's Exhaustive Concordance of the Bible, (Thomas Nelson, 2009).

The Pulpit Commentary, Electronic Database. Copyright © 2001, 2003, 2005, 2006, 2010 by BibleSoft, inc., as quoted at
www.biblehub.com

Vines, Jerry, Vines' Expository Bible Notes, (Thomas Nelson, 2020), as quoted at www.biblegateway.com.

VOICE Bible (Ecclesia Bible Society. 2008).

Webster, Noah, The American Dictionary of the English Language, 1828. as found at https://webstersdictionary1828.com/

Zodhiates, Spiros, ed., The Complete Word Study Dictionary: New Testament (Chattanooga, TN: AMG Publishers, 2000).

Susan Slade and Susie Hale

You have a story.
We want to publish it.

Everyone has as a story to tell. It might be about something you know how to do, or what has happened in your life, or it may be a thrilling, or romantic, or intriguing, or heartwarming, or suspenseful story, starring a cast of characters that have been swimming around in your imagination.

And at Wyatt & Sons Publishers, we can get your story onto the pages of a book just like the one you are holding in your hand. With professional interior design and a custom, professionally designed cover built just for you from the start, you can finally see your dream of being an author become reality. Then, you will see your book listed with retailers all over the world as people are able to buy your book from wherever they are and have it delivered to their home or their e-reader.

So what are you waiting for? This is your time.

visit us at

www.wyattpublishing.com

for details on how to get started becoming a
published author right away.

www.ingramcontent.com/pod-product-compliance
Lightning Source LLC
Chambersburg PA
CBHW070338090426
42733CB00009B/1227